The North African Military Balance

Significant Issues Series
Timely books presenting current CSIS research and analysis of interest to the academic, business, government, and policy communities.
Managing Editor: Roberta Howard Fauriol

About CSIS
In an era of ever-changing global opportunities and challenges, the Center for Strategic and International Studies (CSIS) provides strategic insights and practical policy solutions to decisionmakers. CSIS conducts research and analysis and develops policy initiatives that look into the future and anticipate change.

Founded by David M. Abshire and Admiral Arleigh Burke at the height of the Cold War, CSIS was dedicated to the simple but urgent goal of finding ways for America to survive as a nation and prosper as a people. Since 1962, CSIS has grown to become one of the world's preeminent public policy institutions.

Today, CSIS is a bipartisan, nonprofit organization headquartered in Washington, D.C. More than 220 full-time staff and a large network of affiliated scholars focus their expertise on defense and security; on the world's regions and the unique challenges inherent to them; and on the issues that know no boundary in an increasingly connected world.

Former U.S. senator Sam Nunn became chairman of the CSIS Board of Trustees in 1999, and John J. Hamre has led CSIS as its president and chief executive officer since 2000.

CSIS does not take specific policy positions; accordingly, all views expressed herein should be understood to be solely those of the author(s).

The CSIS Press
Center for Strategic and International Studies
1800 K Street, N.W., Washington, D.C. 20006
Tel: (202) 775-3119   Fax: (202) 775-3199
E-mail: books@csis.org   Web: www.csis.org

The North African Military Balance

Force Developments in the Maghreb

Anthony H. Cordesman and Aram Nerguizian

THE CSIS PRESS

Center for Strategic
and International Studies
Washington, D.C.

Significant Issues Series, Volume 31, Number 2
© 2009 by Center for Strategic and International Studies
Washington, D.C.
Printed on recycled paper in the United States of America
Cover design by Robert L. Wiser, Silver Spring, Md.
Cover image adapted from *The Common-School Geography: An Elementary Treatise on Mathematical, Physical, and Political Geography* by D. M. Warren. Philadelphia: Cowperthwait & Co., 1873.

13 12 11 10 09   5 4 3 2 1

ISSN 0736-7136
ISBN 978-0-89206-552-3

Library of Congress Cataloging-in-Publication Data
Cordesman, Anthony H.
 The North African military balance : force developments in the Maghreb / by Anthony H. Cordesman and Aram Nerguizian.
      p. cm. — (Significant issues series ; v. 31, no. 2)
 Includes bibliographical references.
 ISBN 978-0-89206-552-3 (pbk. : alk. paper) 1. Africa, North—Armed Forces. 2. National security—Africa, North. 3. Africa, North—Defenses. I. Nerguizian, Aram. II. Title. III. Series.

 UA855.55.C67 2009
 355'.033061—dc22

                                        2008039989

CONTENTS

FIGURES

1

INTRODUCTION

There is no military balance in North Africa in the classic sense of the term. Although rivalries and tensions persist between Algeria, Libya, Morocco, and Tunisia, no state in the Maghreb now actively prepares for war with its neighbors, and the prospects of such conflicts are limited at best. Several countries have had border clashes in the past, and there continue to be low-level incidents on the Algerian-Moroccan border, but none of these clashes have approached the point of serious conflict since these countries achieved independence in the 1950s and 1960s.

The Maghreb states only project token forces outside of their immediate border areas. Although several states from the Maghreb have sent symbolic military support to past Arab forces in the Arab-Israeli conflict, such levels of force commitment have had no real military significance. This does not mean, however, that the region has been peaceful. Libya had major regional ambitions in the past and fought a war on its southern border with Chad roughly from 1978 to 1987, but its military adventures largely failed. Despite mass arms purchases in the 1970s and 1980s, Libya has never developed the manpower and support base to use them effectively and has been unable to sustain its arms buys because of economic problems and sanctions. With UN sanctions lifted in 2003, Libya is once again on the market, but its efforts to recapitalize its forces have been minor and major sales and deliveries have yet to materialize.

Morocco's current low-level tensions with Algeria follow a history of more serious border clashes in the past, but none of them were of major military significance. Morocco has fought a war since the mid-1970s to annex the former Spanish Sahara, fighting local indigenous forces known as the Polisario. This has been a low-intensity conflict, although Algeria has provided the Polisario with sanctuary and varying levels of support.

The bloodiest war in the region since independence was a civil conflict. The 1991–2002 Algerian civil war pitted a corrupt military junta hiding behind the façade of an elected government against Islamists, whom the junta deprived of power despite the Islamists' victory in a popular election in the early 1990s. When civil war broke out, violent extremist elements among these Islamists quickly came to dominate the fighting, and the military increasingly relied on equally violent repression. This war has been reduced to a low-level insurgency and counterterrorism campaign, but it has had lingering effects on the regional military balance. The war consumed so many resources that it led to major cuts in Algerian military modernization, although arms purchases rebounded as the military confronted and reduced the Islamist threat.

Today, the military balance in North Africa consists largely of efforts to create military forces that can maintain internal security, defend national borders, and enhance national prestige. Yet, the states of North Africa are also adapting to the threats posed by terrorism, asymmetric warfare, and the proliferation of weapons of mass destruction (WMD). While these are not negligible issues, they are not new challenges.

Libya supported terrorist and extremist movements in the past and has been guilty of state terrorism, but it has ceased such activities in recent years. Despite some of its leaderships' idiosyncrasies, the country has made a successful effort to portray itself as a moderate and pragmatic regime that is primarily interested in economic development and better relations with the West. Libya is also struggling with its own Islamic extremists. Morocco and Tunisia have never supported terrorism or extremism, and Algeria's military junta fought Islamic extremists and terrorists for more than a decade. In the post–September 11 era, Algeria, Libya, Morocco, and Tunisia are facing a common threat from transnational Islamist groups in the Maghreb looking to emulate al Qaeda and al Qaeda in Iraq.

WMD proliferation has also been a problem. Algeria made contingency plans to acquire nuclear weapons in the late 1980s and has also examined options for acquiring long-range missiles. There are some indicators that Algeria still continues to at least examine the options for acquiring nuclear weapons technology. Yet, there is no current evidence that Algeria has implemented major programs to actually acquire these capabilities or to deploy such forces.

Libya has sought chemical and nuclear weapons and long-range missiles, and was reported to have 80 Scud B missile launchers and up to 350–500 missiles as of 2005. It may have also examined options for acquiring biological weapons, but ceased all such efforts in 2003 and opened up its nuclear facilities to inspection by the United States and the International Atomic Energy Agency (IAEA) in 1992.

RESOURCES AND FORCE TRENDS

Patterns in the North African military balance have been erratic at best. The newly independent Maghreb states have followed the same pattern of rapid military buildup that characterized virtually all of the newly independent states in the Near East and Southwest Asia. After the Arab-Israeli conflict in 1973, they embarked on a wasteful military buildup and increased their military forces sharply. This buildup eventually led them to spend more than their national incomes could sustain. In the mid-1980s, military spending began a moderate decline, followed by a sharper decline after the collapse of the Soviet Union. Spending rose again in the late 1990s and spiked with major acquisitions by Algeria and Morocco starting in 2006. Libya may also see major deliveries starting in 2009 if its $2.5 billion deal with Russia is solidified.

- **Figure 1.1** provides a summary comparison of the present strength of Algerian, Libyan, Moroccan, and Tunisian military forces. (Figures 1.1 –1.12 appear at the end of this chapter.)

- **Figure 1.2** shows the trends in military expenditures and arms imports in constant U.S. dollars. The massive decline in spending after the mid-1980s is clearly apparent, as is the fact that arms imports have dropped far more quickly than military expenditures. The rise in military expenditures in the late 1990s was driven largely by the Algerian civil war and low-intensity conflict between Morocco and the Polisario. These events help explain why arms imports remained comparatively low through the early 2000s and why military modernization was badly undercapitalized for more than a decade. Spending began rising once again in 2003, however, as Algeria and Morocco sought to offer contracts for upgrades and new systems.

- **Figure 1.3** shows the same trends in terms of military effort as a percentage of gross national product (GNP) and as a percentage of central government expenditures, and arms imports as a percentage of total imports and of total population. Although the North African states failed to properly capitalize their military forces, they have significantly reduced the impact of military spending on their economies, national budgets, and imports.

- **Figure 1.4** shows the more recent trends in military expenditures in constant U.S. dollars, drawn from a different source. Algeria clearly dominates regional military spending, driven in part by its civil war and in part by the ambitions and bureaucratic momentum of its ruling military junta as fueled by oil and gas exports. Morocco has maintained high spending levels largely because of the continuing costs of its war with the Polisario. Libyan military spending has continued to decline because of the impact of its economic problems and past U.S. and UN sanctions. Tunisia has never attempted to build up major military forces.

- **Figure 1.5** shows how the regional trends in North African arms imports compared with those in other regions between 1985 and 1999. North Africa was clearly never a significant part of the world arms trade in spite of the ambitions of several regional states.

- **Figure 1.6** highlights the sharp decline in arms imports as a percentage of total imports. On one hand, this decline reveals a significant drop in the impact of arms imports on local economies. On the other hand, it illustrates just how sharply North African states—none of which has significant domestic military industries—have undercapitalized the modernization of their military forces.

- **Figure 1.7** provides more current data on new arms orders and deliveries. The data show that recent Algerian new orders have increased consistently and that significant arms deliveries took place between 1996 and 2006. Libya experienced a fairly consistent precipitous decline in arms orders and deliveries during the 1992–2003 period, although this trend may now be reversed as the result of the lifting of sanctions and new orders from Russia and the European Union. Morocco shows a less steep decline, and Tunisia shows an increase in deliveries during 1996–1999, although the amounts involved are so small that they scarcely constitute a military buildup.

- **Figure 1.8** shows recent arms imports by supplier country. Morocco and Tunisia are the only countries that have received U.S. arms after 1996 and Tunisia has not made any recent orders. Morocco has depended largely on Europe for its arms, although new orders dropped sharply between 1991 and 2003, before increasing again in 2003–2006. Libya has only placed limited orders, and has not placed significant orders with any country capable of supplying it with the most-advanced weapons. It did step up its new orders during 2003–2006, however, reflecting an easing of UN sanctions and its ability to import arms from developing countries that are less careful about UN sanctions. Algeria has relied largely on Russia and Eastern Europe, and placed significant new orders during 2003–2006.

- **Figure 1.9** highlights just how serious the decline in Libyan military efforts was between the mid-1980s and 2007, revealing a sharp imbalance between continued military spending and inadequate arms imports throughout most of the 1990s.

- **Figures 1.10** and **1.11** reveal other imbalances in North African military efforts. Most countries have maintained larger manpower and equipment pools than they could afford to sustain. All of the Maghreb states except Tunisia bought more military equipment during the 1970s and 1980s than they can now adequately support. Like many less developed countries, the Maghreb states confused weapons numbers and the "glitter factor" of buying advanced weapons technology with military effectiveness. Algeria, Libya, and Morocco saturated their military forces with weaponry between 1972 and 1985 without buying proper support, sustainability, and command, control, communications, computers, and intelligence (C⁴I) equipment. They created teeth-to-tail ratios that are about 2–3 times the proper ratio for military effectiveness.

- **Figure 1.12** shows the most recent data on North Africa military manpower by service. Notably, the training and equipment levels for almost all of the reserve forces in the Maghreb countries are so low that manpower numbers have little real military value. Algeria's force structure reflects a heavy emphasis on the para-military forces needed to fight its civil war. Morocco's large army reflects the need to maintain large forces to protect the south from Polisario attacks. As later figures show, Libya has very low manning levels for its total equipment holdings. Tunisia's distribution of military manpower is what might be expected of a small and defensive military power.

The cumulative message of these figures is that the force structures of Algeria, Libya, and Morocco grew to a point at which their economies can no longer provide the funding for the equipment, manpower, training, logistics, infrastructure, and sustainability necessary to make these force structures effective. This overexpansion of the total force structure was particularly severe in the case of Libya, which sized its forces based on its peak oil revenues in 1981 and 1982, when it spent more than 12 percent of its GNP on its military forces. Libya has never been able to find the resources or manpower to use more than one-half of the equipment that it bought, and cut military spending to around 5–6 percent of its GNP after 1993.[1] This imbalance resulted in substantial waste, and many purchases were rendered nearly useless by the lack of proper support. The end result has been that several nations have let portions of their older equipment become inoperable or obsolete. Algeria and Libya are only spending a small fraction of their military budget on the modernization that is necessary to recapitalize their forces.

The Maghreb states have seen conscription, and the expansion of military manpower, as a useful means of providing employment and ensuring the loyalty of their youth. These efforts at nation building have complemented a similar expansion of national civil service and employment in the state sector of the economy. This approach helped lead to overexpansion of their forces during the early 1980s and the creation of large armies filled with poorly trained men who received little useful training or education while in military service. The cost of maintaining large pools of military manpower contributed to diminished economic growth during the early and mid-1980s, and this situation has continued ever since in spite of cuts in total manning since that time.

The military value of conscription is dubious for other reasons. Conscript service is often touted as a form of education and nation building. In practice, it has helped disguise unemployment, but the preparation conscripts actually receive has little value in terms of training or education. Conscript service has also proven to do little to win the loyalty of young men, aid in internal stability, or serve the cause of nation building. It has often been either a source of added alienation or schooling in propaganda and repression.

Like most developing countries, the Maghreb states have long underfunded advanced training and the other aspects of manpower quality for their full-time and career forces. None of the Maghreb states have maintained average military expenditures per man in uniform at a high enough level to maintain effective manpower quality and retain technically trained soldiers. Morocco and Tunisia have done better than the others in improving manpower quality. All of the Maghreb states have had serious problems adapting their military organization and discipline to account for the need for far more skilled junior officers and noncommissioned officers, and have demonstrated poor management of military personnel and career structures.

Several detailed national developments have helped shape the trends in Figures 1.1 through 1.12:

- Algeria has a force structure of more than six active division equivalents, with a total army manpower of only 127,000 men, 80,000 of which are poorly trained conscripts. In addition, it has six military regions that require military manpower. This force structure has sharply overstretched its army and made effective force planning impossible. The situation has been made worse by rampant corruption at the highest levels of the Algerian officer corps.

- Algeria did a relatively good job of buying armor before its civil war begin in the late 1980s, but it spent too much on artillery quantity and too little on artillery and infantry mobility and quality. It bought a poor mix of relatively low-quality anti-tank weapons and air defense systems. Since that time, it has increased its paramilitary forces to more than 187,200 men to deal with its civil war, compounding all of its military planning, force structure, and force modernization problems.

- The Algerian Air Force has only bought a limited number of modern air defense fighters for its force, possessing a total of only 141 combat aircraft and 33 armed helicopters, including 34 Su-24 and six modern Su-30MK attack aircraft. It has long sought to buy new aircraft, however, and will be receiving a total of 28 Su-30MKs by 2010. Its surface-to-air missile (SAM) defenses employ technology from the early to late 1970s and are now vulnerable to commercially available electronic warfare capabilities and to any force with modern anti-radiation missiles. These too will be updated by new S-300PMU-2 heavy SAM batteries.

- Until the late 1980s, Algeria gave its more advanced units with heavy armor and advanced aircraft adequate funding, but it sharply underfunded its overall manpower and support structure. Since the late 1980s, it has had to concentrate its resources on fighting a steadily intensifying civil war, forcing it to sharply underfund its equipment modernization. In the post–civil war era, a strategy has yet to emerge to provide regular forces with the resources they need to be effective in combat beyond select units.

- Tunisia has provided reasonable wages for its career officers, but has done little to turn its many 12-month conscripts into effective soldiers.

- Libya has invested in equipment and facilities rather than a sound manpower, infrastructure, and support base. Its poorly trained conscripts and "volunteers" suffered a decisive defeat in Chad at the hands of lightly armed Chadian forces during the conflict between the two states. Its forces have since declined in quality.

- Libya's military equipment purchases have been chaotic. During the Cold War and the period before Libya was placed under UN sanctions, its arms buys involved incredible waste and overexpenditure on equipment. These decisions were made without regard to providing adequate manpower and support forces and did not reflect a clear concept of force development or combined arms.

- Libya's adventures in trying to influence events in other states and its disastrous military intervention in Chad involved comparatively little actual use of Libya's total forces. Libya did, however, have a powerful catalytic effect on the military buildup of other states in the region. As bad as Libya's military forces were, no neighbor could ignore a vast pool of military equipment. Yet, ties with its neighbors are warmer than they were in the past, and Libya has begun to participate in NATO naval exercises and shares common counterterrorism and counterinsurgency objectives.

- Libya has to keep many of its aircraft and more than 1,200 of its tanks in storage. Its other army equipment purchases require far more manpower than its small active army and low-quality reserves can provide. Its overall ratio of weapons to manpower is militarily absurd, and Libya has compounded its problems by buying a wide diversity of equipment types that make it impossible to create an effective training and support base.

- Morocco's continuing low-level tensions with Algeria and Mauritania and its nearly two decade–long war with the Polisario over the control of Western Sahara are the key factors shaping its force trends. It is interesting to note, however, that Morocco's arms purchases were not particularly well suited to dealing with a low-level guerrilla threat until 1982–1983. As late as 1992, Morocco's combat engineering efforts reflected a sounder pattern of purchases for dealing with the Polisario than did its weapons buys. These problems were partly the result of the fact that the Moroccan Army was still focusing on a possible confrontation with Algeria rather than on the conflict with the Polisario.

- Morocco then spent much of its money on maintaining a force of 100,000–150,000 men in the Spanish Sahara. This force became relatively capable by the early 1990s and has effectively defeated its opposition. Morocco still is unable to fund adequate force modernization, however, and has bought so many different types of major land weapons over the years that it is difficult to keep its support costs at reasonable levels, to provide proper training, and to maintain suitable C^{4}I battle-management capability.

■ Morocco has maintained a higher real average of spending per man in its career forces than that of the other Maghreb states, but it still underfunds and undertrains its conscripts and enlisted men.

■ The Moroccan Air Force has a better balance of equipment type than its land forces or naval forces. Nevertheless, Morocco still relies on obsolescent F-5s and Mirages F-1s, and its purchase of French and U.S. combat aircraft has increased its training and support problems. Morocco also has no meaningful SAM defenses.

■ Tunisia began to acquire modern armor and fighter aircraft in 1985 but still has bought only limited numbers of weapons. It has done a reasonably good job of expanding its army and air force, but its force size and equipment holdings are inadequate for combat with either of its larger neighbors. Its holdings also include too many types of equipment to allow for effective organization and support.

■ Money still severely limits the size and modernization of the Tunisian force structure. As of early 2008, it had only 35,800 actives, of which 27,000 were conscripts. Its only modern armored vehicles consisted of 54 M-60A3 main battle tanks (MBTs) 30 older M-60A1 MBTs, and 140 M-113 armored personnel carriers. It had no self-propelled (SP) artillery, and its most modern aircraft consisted of 12 aging F-5E/Fs. It had no modern attack helicopters and no major SAMs.

NOTES

1. For further details, see various editions of the U.S. Department of State, *World Military Expenditures and Arms Transfers*; the annual International Institute for Strategic Studies' *Military Balance*; and the annual reports by Richard F. Grimmett of the Congressional Research Service entitled "Conventional Arms Transfers to Developing Nations."

Figure 1.1 Algerian, Libyan, Moroccan, and Tunisian Forces, 2008

Category/Weapon	Algeria	Libya	Morocco	Tunisia
MANPOWER				
Total Active	147,000	76,000	195,800	35,800
(Conscripts)	80,000	25,000	100,000	22,000
Total Regular	67,000	51,000	95,800	13,800
Royal/Special Guard and Other	0	-	1,500	-
Total Reserve	150,000	40,000	150,000	-
Total Active and Reserve	297,000	116,000	345,800	35,800
Paramilitary	187,200	-	50,000	12,000
LAND FORCES				
Active Manpower	127,000	50,000	175,000	27,000
(Conscripts)	80,000	25,000	100,000	22,000
Reserve Manpower	150,000	-	150,000	-
Total Manpower	277,000	50,000	325,000	27,000
Main Battle Tanks	895	800 (1,225)	380 (200)	84
AIFVs/Armored Cars/Lt. Tanks	1,040	1,000+	186	48
APCs/Recces/Scouts/Half-Tracks	840	1,065	1,149	328
ATGM Launchers	200+	3,000	790	590
SP Artillery	170	444	199	0
Towed Artillery	375	647+	118	115
MRLs	144	830	35	0
Mortars	330	500	1,706	161
SSM Launchers	-	45	0	0
AA Guns	875	490	407	127
Lt. SAM Launchers	288+	424+*	107	86
AIR & AIR DEFENSE FORCES				
Active Manpower	14,000	18,000	13,000	4,000
(Air Defense Only)	N/A	-	-	-
Reserve Manpower	-	-	-	-
(Air Defense Only)	N/A	-	-	-
Aircraft				
Total Fighters/FGA/Recces	141	349	72	15
Bombers	0	7	0	0
Fighters	55	229	19	12
FGA	78	113	47	3
COIN/OCU	-	-	-	6
Recces	8	7	6	0
Airborne Early Warning (AEW/EW)	0	0	4	0
Maritime Reconnaissance	6	0	0	0
Combat-Capable Trainers	49	250	19	0
Tankers	6	0	3	0
Transport	38	85+	44	20

(continued)

Figure 1.1 (continued)

Category/Weapon	Algeria	Libya	Morocco	Tunisia
Helicopters				
Attack/Armed/ASW	33	35	19	0
Other	142	101	73	43
Total	175	136	92	43
SAM Forces				
Batteries	3	15+	0	0
Heavy Launchers	140+	216+	0	0
Medium Launchers	-	-	-	-
AA Guns	725	some	-	-
NAVAL FORCES				
Active Manpower	6,000	8,000	7,800	4,800
Regular Navy	6,000	8,000	6,300	4,800
Naval Guards	-	-	-	-
Marines	-	-	1,500	-
Reserve Manpower	-	-	-	-
Total Active & Reserve Manpower	6,000	8,000	7,800	4,800
Submarines	2	2	0	0
Destroyers/Frigates/Corvettes	9	3	3	0
Missile	9	3	3	0
Other	0	0	0	0
Missile Patrol	9	14	4	12
Coastal/Inshore Patrol	11	4	23	13
Mine	0	4	0	0
Amphibious Ships	3	4	4	0
Landing Craft/Light Support	13	16	8	6
MPA/ASW/Combat Helicopter	0	7	3	0

*Extensive but unknown amounts inoperable or in storage.

Source: Adapted by Anthony H. Cordesman from data provided by U.S. experts, and from the
   International Institute for Strategic Studies, *The Military Balance,* various editions, http://www
   .iiss.org/publications/military-balance/.
Note: Figures in parentheses are additional equipment in storage. SSM launchers are major systems.
   The number for total fighters/FGA/Recces is not the same as the total number of combat-
   capable aircraft. "0" connotes that a zero number has been verified, whereas "-" connotes that
   data are not known or verifiable.

Figure 1.2 Algerian, Libyan, Moroccan, and Tunisian Spending, 1985–2007 (constant US$2008 billions)

North African military expenditures and arms transfers have dropped to low levels by global standards

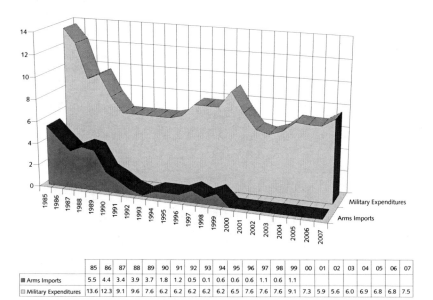

	85	86	87	88	89	90	91	92	93	94	95	96	97	98	99	00	01	02	03	04	05	06	07
■ Arms Imports	5.5	4.4	3.4	3.9	3.7	1.8	1.2	0.5	0.1	0.6	0.6	0.6	1.1	0.6	1.1								
□ Military Expenditures	13.6	12.3	9.1	9.6	7.6	6.2	6.2	6.2	6.2	6.2	6.5	7.6	7.6	7.6	9.1	7.3	5.9	5.6	6.0	6.9	6.8	6.8	7.5

Source: Adapted by Anthony H. Cordesman from data from the U.S. Department of State, *World Military Expenditures and Arms Transfers,* various editions; International Institute for Strategic Studies, *The Military Balance,* various editions.

Note: Figures rounded up to the closest $100 million. Arms imports data for 2000–2007 not available.

Figure 1.3 North African Military Efforts as a Percentage of GNP, Government Expenditures, Imports, and Total Population, 1985–2007

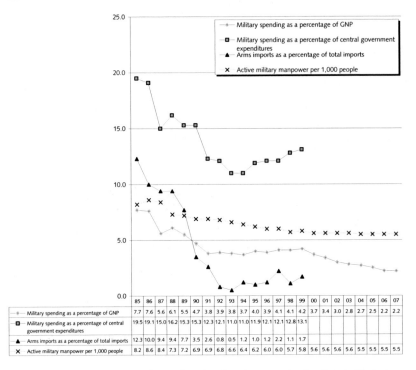

	85	86	87	88	89	90	91	92	93	94	95	96	97	98	99	00	01	02	03	04	05	06	07
Military spending as a percentage of GNP	7.7	7.6	5.6	6.1	5.5	4.7	3.8	3.9	3.8	3.7	4.0	3.9	4.1	4.1	4.2	3.7	3.4	3.0	2.8	2.7	2.5	2.2	2.2
Military spending as a percentage of central government expenditures	19.5	19.1	15.0	16.2	15.3	15.3	12.3	12.1	11.0	11.0	11.9	12.1	12.1	12.8	13.1								
Arms imports as a percentage of total imports	12.3	10.0	9.4	9.4	7.7	3.5	2.6	0.8	0.5	1.2	1.0	1.2	2.2	1.1	1.7								
Active military manpower per 1,000 people	8.2	8.6	8.4	7.3	7.2	6.9	6.9	6.8	6.6	6.4	6.2	6.0	6.0	5.7	5.8	5.6	5.6	5.6	5.6	5.5	5.5	5.5	5.5

Source: Adapted by Anthony H. Cordesman from data from the International Institute for Strategic Studies, *The Military Balance,* various editions; U.S. Department of State, *World Military Expenditures and Arms Transfers*, various editions.

Note: Arms imports data and military spending as percentage of central government expenditures data for 2000–2007 not available.

Figure 1.4 North African Military Expenditures by Country, 1997–2006 (constant US$2008 millions)

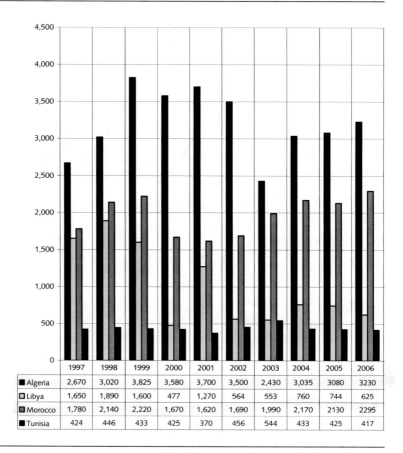

	1997	1998	1999	2000	2001	2002	2003	2004	2005	2006
■ Algeria	2,670	3,020	3,825	3,580	3,700	3,500	2,430	3,035	3080	3230
☐ Libya	1,650	1,890	1,600	477	1,270	564	553	760	744	625
▨ Morocco	1,780	2,140	2,220	1,670	1,620	1,690	1,990	2,170	2130	2295
■ Tunisia	424	446	433	425	370	456	544	433	425	417

Source: Adapted by Anthony Cordesman from the International Institute for Strategic Studies, *The Military Balance*, various editions.

Note: The International Institute for Strategic Studies (IISS) does not report military expenditures, but it does report military budget, which does not include any procurement costs.

Figure 1.5 North African Arms Deliveries, 1985–1999 (constant US$1999 billions)

North African arms deliveries declined and constituted a minor portion of the world market

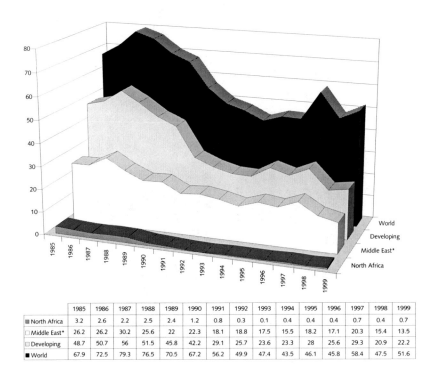

	1985	1986	1987	1988	1989	1990	1991	1992	1993	1994	1995	1996	1997	1998	1999
■ North Africa	3.2	2.6	2.2	2.5	2.4	1.2	0.8	0.3	0.1	0.4	0.4	0.4	0.7	0.4	0.7
□ Middle East*	26.2	26.2	30.2	25.6	22	22.3	18.1	18.8	17.5	15.5	18.2	17.1	20.3	15.4	13.5
□ Developing	48.7	50.7	56	51.5	45.8	42.2	29.1	25.7	23.6	23.3	28	25.6	29.3	20.9	22.2
■ World	67.9	72.5	79.3	76.5	70.5	67.2	56.2	49.9	47.4	43.5	46.1	45.8	58.4	47.5	51.6

*Middle East does not include North African states other than Egypt.
Source: Adapted by Anthony H. Cordesman from the U.S. Department of State, *World Military Expenditures and Arms Transfers,* various editions.

Figure 1.6 North African Arms Imports as a Percentage of Total Imports, 1985–1999

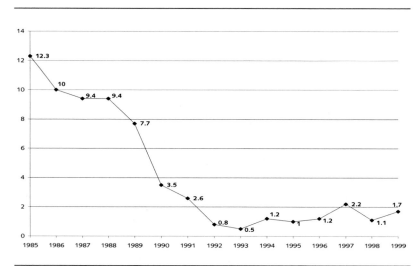

Source: Adapted by Anthony H. Cordesman from the U.S. Department of State, *World Military Expenditures and Arms Transfers,* various editions.
Note: North Africa does not include Egypt.

Figure 1.7 New North African Arms Agreements and Deliveries by Importing
Country, 1987–2006 (in current US$ millions)

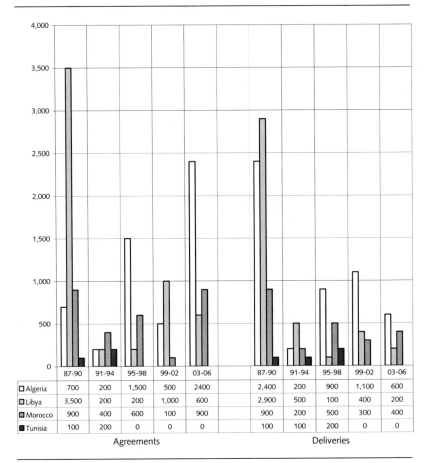

	87-90	91-94	95-98	99-02	03-06	87-90	91-94	95-98	99-02	03-06
☐ Algeria	700	200	1,500	500	2400	2,400	200	900	1,100	600
☐ Libya	3,500	200	200	1,000	600	2,900	500	100	400	200
☐ Morocco	900	400	600	100	900	900	200	500	300	400
■ Tunisia	100	200	0	0	0	100	100	200	0	0
			Agreements					Deliveries		

Source: Adapted by Anthony H. Cordesman from Richard F. Grimmett, *Conventional Arms Transfers
    to Developing Nations,* various editions.
Note: 0 = data less than $50 million or nil. All data rounded to the nearest $100 million.

Figure 1.8 New North African Arms Orders by Supplier Country, 1987–2006 (in current US$ millions)

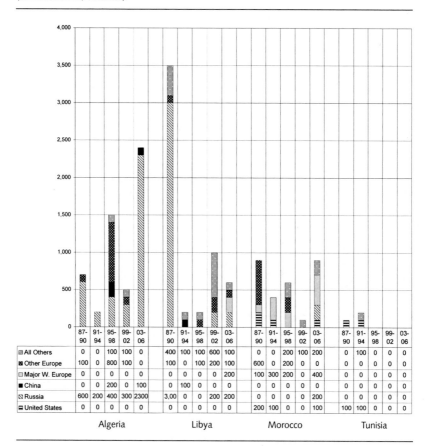

	Algeria 87-90	91-94	95-98	99-02	03-06	Libya 87-90	91-94	95-98	99-02	03-06	Morocco 87-90	91-94	95-98	99-02	03-06	Tunisia 87-90	91-94	95-98	99-02	03-06
All Others	0	0	100	100	0	400	100	100	600	100	0	0	200	100	200	0	100	0	0	0
Other Europe	100	0	800	100	0	100	0	100	200	100	600	0	200	0	0	0	0	0	0	0
Major W. Europe	0	0	0	0	0	0	0	0	0	200	100	300	200	0	400	0	0	0	0	0
China	0	0	200	0	100	0	100	0	0	0	0	0	0	0	0	0	0	0	0	0
Russia	600	200	400	300	2300	3,00	0	0	200	200	0	0	0	0	200	0	0	0	0	0
United States	0	0	0	0	0	0	0	0	0	0	200	100	0	0	100	100	100	0	0	0

Source: Adapted by Anthony H. Cordesman from Richard F. Grimmett, *Conventional Arms Transfers to Developing Nations,* various editions.
Note: 0 = less than $50 million or nil. All data rounded to the nearest $100 million.

Figure 1.9 Libyan Spending and Arms Imports, 1986–2007 (constant US$2008 millions)

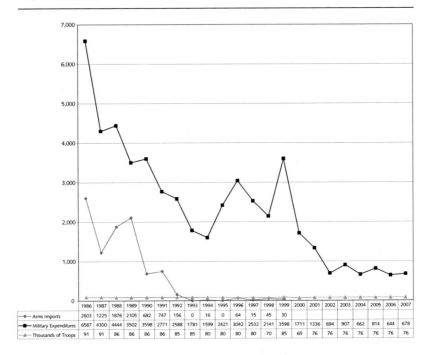

	1986	1987	1988	1989	1990	1991	1992	1993	1994	1995	1996	1997	1998	1999	2000	2001	2002	2003	2004	2005	2006	2007
Arms Imports	2603	1225	1876	2105	682	747	156	0	16	0	64	15	45	30								
Military Expenditures	6587	4300	4444	3502	3598	2771	2588	1781	1599	2421	3042	2532	2141	3598	1711	1336	694	907	662	814	644	678
Thousands of Troops	91	91	86	86	86	86	85	85	80	80	80	80	70	85	65	76	76	76	76	76	76	76

Source: Adapted by Anthony H. Cordesman from U.S. Department of State, *World Military Expenditures and Arms Transfers,* various editions. Some data adjusted or estimated by author.
Note: Arms imports data for 2000–2007 not available.

Figure 1.10 Trends in Total North African Military Manpower (Algerian, Libyan, Moroccan, and Tunisian military manpower in thousands)

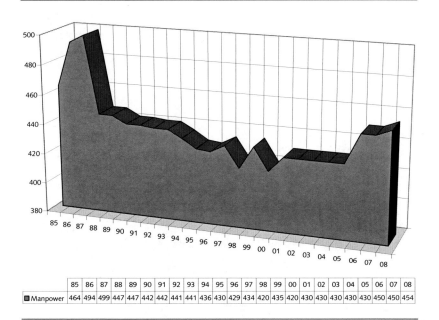

	85	86	87	88	89	90	91	92	93	94	95	96	97	98	99	00	01	02	03	04	05	06	07	08
▣ Manpower	464	494	499	447	447	442	442	441	441	436	430	429	434	420	435	420	430	430	430	430	430	450	450	454

Source: Adapted by Anthony H. Cordesman from the International Institute for Strategic Studies, *The Military Balance,* various editions; U.S. Department of State, *World Military Expenditures and Arms Transfers,* various editions.

Figure 1.11 Total Manpower in North African Military Forces, 2008

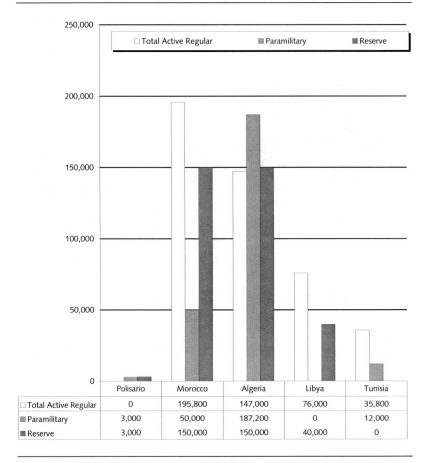

	Polisario	Morocco	Algeria	Libya	Tunisia
☐ Total Active Regular	0	195,800	147,000	76,000	35,800
▨ Paramilitary	3,000	50,000	187,200	0	12,000
▨ Reserve	3,000	150,000	150,000	40,000	0

Source: Adapted by Anthony H. Cordesman from the International Institute for Strategic Studies, *The Military Balance,* various editions.

Figure 1.12 Total Regular Military Manpower in North African Forces by Service, 2008

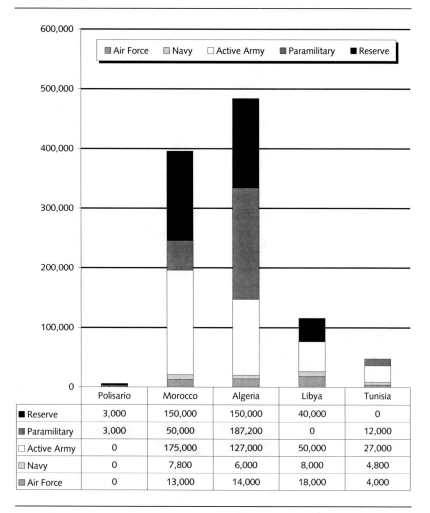

	Polisario	Morocco	Algeria	Libya	Tunisia
■ Reserve	3,000	150,000	150,000	40,000	0
▩ Paramilitary	3,000	50,000	187,200	0	12,000
☐ Active Army	0	175,000	127,000	50,000	27,000
▨ Navy	0	7,800	6,000	8,000	4,800
▨ Air Force	0	13,000	14,000	18,000	4,000

Source: Adapted by Anthony H. Cordesman from the International Institute for Strategic Studies, *The Military Balance,* various editions.

2

THE MILITARY FORCES OF MOROCCO

Morocco's forces are shaped by the fact that its only major external threat, Algeria, no longer presents a significant risk. Its military spending is driven largely by its war with Polisario for control of Western Sahara and by factors such as bureaucratic momentum, regional rivalries with Algeria and Spain, and the country's search for status and prestige. This spending consumes some 3–4 percent of Morocco's gross domestic product and 11–12 percent of its national budget. These percentages are not high by regional standards, but Morocco has a sharply rising population, massive unemployment, and a desperate need for resources for economic development. Military spending and the war in Western Sahara are a major burden on the country.

The trends in Moroccan military forces are shown in **Figure 2.1**. Morocco's military forces and budget have increased steadily since 1985, with a large jump in expenditures between 1985 and 1990 during its war with the Polisario. Morocco's total manpower and land forces shot up during that period as well. Total manpower increased from 149,000 in 1985 to 192,500 in 1990, and its land forces rose from 130,000 men to 175,000 men in the same period. Since 1990, there have been only limited changes in total force size.

In 2008, Morocco had a total of 195,800 actives and 150,000 army reserves. Its land forces had an inventory of 580 MBTs, 70 armored infantry fighting vehicles (AIFVs), 765 armored personnel carriers (APCs), 199 SP artillery, 118 towed artillery, and 35 multiple rocket launchers (MRLs). Its air forces had a total of 89 combat-capable aircraft and 19 attack helicopters. Its navy possessed three major surface ships, four missile patrol craft, 23 other patrol craft, and four amphibious ships.

MOROCCAN ARMY

The 175,000-man Moroccan Army is the only force in the Maghreb that has had to train and organize for serious conventional combat since the 1960s. Yet, most of its combat experience has consisted of a form of irregular warfare roughly similar to how Algeria and Libya have had to fight Islamist terrorists and extremists. The army is organized into two major commands: Northern Zone (Rabat) and Southern Zone (Agadir). The Northern Zone deals largely with defense of the Algerian border and internal security. The Southern Zone is organized to fight the Polisario. The order of battle changes to deploy the forces necessary to deal with the threat in Western Sahara at any given time, but the bulk of the army was deployed to the Southern Zone in early 2008.

The army has three mechanized infantry brigade headquarters, one light security brigade, two paratrooper brigades, and eight mechanized/motorized infantry regiments (with 2–3 battalions each). It also has an exceptionally large number of small independent units. These include 12 armored battalions, 35 infantry battalions, three motorized (camel corps) battalions, one mountain battalion, 11 artillery battalions, one air defense group, seven engineering battalions, four commando units, and two airborne battalions.[1]

The Moroccan Army has a significant number of conscripts as well as a strong cadre of experienced regulars. Morocco's large population and low per capita income have led many poorer Moroccans to pursue military careers. The pay and benefits are adequate and living conditions are acceptable, even in the camps and strong points in the south. Tactical doctrine still relies heavily on French and Spanish experience, but U.S. influence is growing and Morocco benefits from U.S. military advisers. Moroccan army trainers operate throughout the region. Yet, Moroccan army training is still erratic and much of it is conducted at the unit level, resulting in very different levels of effectiveness depending on the particular unit involved.

A 150,000-man reserve exists on paper, but—as is the case with virtually all of the reserve forces in the Middle East—most of this manpower serves little real purpose. Reserve training is minimal, and there are few combat ready officers, other ranks, and specialists with the kind of current war-fighting skills that the army would need in war. The only combat effective reserves would be men called back to units that they had recently left.

The paramilitary Force Auxiliaire is probably more effective. This 30,000-man force designed to reinforce the army in a campaign against Algeria could provide service support and rear area security. It also includes the 5,000-man Mobile Intervention Corps, which is fully equipped with light armored vehicles and Land Rovers and automatic and crew-served weapons. The Force Auxiliaire has also been used successfully in rear-area security operations against the Polisario.

The Gendarmerie Royale is a 20,000-man support force headquartered in Rabat that serves a wide range of state security functions. It has heavy elements that can deal with major internal security threats. Its order of battle includes a coast-guard unit, a paratrooper squadron, a paramilitary brigade with four mobile groups, and one air squadron.

The army is deployed to concentrate Morocco's armored forces in the North and a large anti-guerrilla force in the south. This focus reflects its longstanding emphasis on deterring Algeria while fighting the Polisario. There is one Royal Guard battalion, a mountain battalion, an armored squadron, a mechanized squadron, a cavalry squadron, and an artillery group in the Northwest Atlas mountain range. The border is defended by two mechanized infantry regiments, three infantry battalions, one camel corps battalion, two armored squadrons, and one artillery group.

There are normally three mechanized infantry brigades, nine mechanized infantry regiments, 25 infantry battalions, two paratrooper battalions, two camel corps battalions, four armored squadrons (with UR-416 APCs), and seven artillery groups in the south. Morocco also plays a significant peacekeeping role. Morocco's troop contributions to UN forces include 724 men in Ivory Coast, 809 men in the Democratic Republic of Congo, and 229 men in Serbia. Morocco also deployed 5,000 men to the United Arab Emirates during the Persian Gulf War, including a 700-man paratrooper unit.

Morocco's 200 M-48A5, 220 M-60A1, 120 M-60A3, and 40 T-72 MBTs have given the army adequate heavy armor. Yet, most of the M-48A5s remain in storage. Morocco also has an additional 111 SK-105 Kuerassier and five AMX-13 light tanks, but these are obsolescent.

Overall levels of tank training range from limited to adequate, and Morocco only conducts limited maneuver and large-unit training.

Reports differ as to the strength and types of other fighting vehicles in Moroccan forces, but its armored reconnaissance strength seems to include 40 EBR-75s, 80 AMX-10s, 190 AML-90s, 38 AML-60s, and 20 M-1114s. It also has 30 Ratel 20s, 30 Ratel 90s, and 10 AMX-10Ps employed as AIFVs. Its APCs include 400 M-113A1s, 45 VAB-VCIs, and 320 VAB-VTTs. It may also have 45 OT-62 and OT-64 APCs.

This diverse mix of armored fighting vehicles and APCs is in many cases of mediocre quality and readiness and lacks effective standardization. Morocco's emphasis on AIFVs and APCs does, however, reflect a response to the special needs imposed by its terrain and to its experience in fighting the Polisario. Although Algeria poses a somewhat theoretical threat of armored warfare, Morocco has had to fight the Polisario largely using mechanized and light infantry.

Morocco is well equipped with artillery. As of mid-2008, it has 118 towed weapons, including 30 L-118 and 20 M-101 105-mm weapons, 18 M-46 130-mm weapons, 30 FH-70s, and 20 M-1141 55-mm weapons. It has 199 SP weapons: five Mk 61 105-mm howitzers, 90 AMX-F3 and 44 M-109A1/B 155-mm howitzers, and 60 M-110 203-mm howitzers. It also has 35 BM-21 MRLs and some 1,700 81-mm, 106-mm, and 120-mm mortars. Roughly 570 of the mortars are 120-mm weapons, 20 of which are mounted on VAB armored vehicles. Morocco also has 32–36 106-mm SP M-106A2s.

This artillery strength does not match Algeria's, but it includes a large number of modern SP weapons. Morocco seems to be able to operate most of its artillery weapons effectively as individual units, but it has problems with combined arms, artillery maneuver, and beyond visual range targeting. In August 2007, the U.S. Defense Security and Cooperation Agency (DSCA) notified Congress of a possible sale under the Foreign Military Sale (FMS) program of 60 M109A5 155-mm SP howitzers to Morocco to augment its existing artillery force.[2]

Morocco's holdings of anti-tank weapons include 440 M-47 Dragon, 80 Milan, 150 BGM-71A TOW and 40 AT-3 9K11 Sagger anti-tank guided missile (ATGM) launchers. Roughly 80 of the TOWs are mounted on M-901 armored vehicles. Its other anti-tank weapons include eight 100-mm SU-100 SP guns, 28 90-mm M-56 towed guns, 500 66-mm M-72 light anti-tank weapons, 200 89-mm M-20 rocket launchers, and some 350 M-40A1 106-mm recoilless rifles.

Morocco has some 407 antiaircraft guns, including 150–180 ZPU-2 and 20 ZPU-4 14.5-mm guns, 40 M-167 and 60 M-163 Vulcan SP 20-mm guns, 75–90 ZU-23-2 23-mm guns, and 17 KS-19 towed 100-mm guns. It also has 37 M-48 Chaparral SP SAM launchers and 70 SA-7 Grails. In 2004, Morocco placed an order for the Tunguska-M1 gun/missile short-to-medium range SP air defense system with Russia's arms export entity Rosoboronexport.[3] Estimated at $100 million at the time, the order's completion cannot be verified.

The army's war-fighting effectiveness is mixed. It is most experienced in dealing with light infantry and guerilla forces such as the Polisario and is best trained and organized for defense against this kind of warfare. Although Morocco has some outstanding battalion-sized elements, most of its heavy armor lacks proper support equipment, technical manpower, and spares. Morocco does not conduct serious large-unit armored maneuver training and lacks the service support and sustaining capability it needs to fight a prolonged conflict with Algeria. Its artillery is effective against infantry and slow-moving forces but lacks proficiency in combined arms and armored maneuver speed. Logistic support, however, is adequate, and Morocco has shown that it can maintain an adequate supply line over considerable distances.

MOROCCAN NAVY

The 7,800-man Moroccan Navy is a relatively large force by local standards, although it scarcely makes Morocco a major Mediterranean or Atlantic naval power. It has three frigates, four missile fast attack craft, 17 large coastal patrol craft, six inshore patrol craft, four amphibious landing craft, four support ships, and 44 customs and coast-guard vessels. In addition, 1,500 men are organized in two marine naval infantry battalions.

The navy is based in Agadir, Al Hoceima, Casablanca, Dakhla, and Tangier. Casablanca is its headquarters and the key port. Agadir and Dakhla are the main secondary bases on the Atlantic, and Al Hoceima is the key secondary base on the Mediterranean. Morocco plans to construct an additional major naval base at Qsar es-Seghir between Tangier and the Spanish province of Ceuta. This base is expected to be commissioned in 2010 and will facilitate navy operations near the Strait of Gibraltar, guard a possible Tangier-Med container terminal, and augment Morocco's ability to adequately contribute to NATO's naval counterinsurgency operations in the Mediterranean.[4] In addition to the navy's resources and basing, the Ministry of Fisheries operates 11 Pilatus Britten-Norman defender maritime surveillance aircraft.[5]

As of 2008, the navy had two French-made Mohammed V-class frigates (French Floreal-class): the *Mohammed V* and the *Hassan II*, commissioned in 2002 and 2003, respectively. Each had four Exocet ship-to-ship missiles, two Matra Simbad SAM launchers, a 76-mm gun, Mk 46 torpedoes, and two 375-mm anti-ship marine mortars. They also had electronic support measures and chaff and infrared (IR) flare launchers. They have modern Thompson air/surface search radars and can carry one AS-565SA Panther helicopter. Their anti-submarine warfare sonar capabilities were unclear.

The navy also had one 1,480-ton modified Descubierta-class guided-missile frigate, named the *Lt. Colonel Errhamani*, commissioned in 1983, and refitted in Spain in 1996. The ship had four MM-38 Exocet launchers (sea-skimming missiles with semi-active radar guidance, a range of 42 km, and a 165-kg warhead), an octuple Aspide launcher (semi-active radar homing to 13 km at Mach 2.5), one 76-mm gun, six 324-mm torpedo tubes, and antisubmarine mortars. The navy rarely loaded Exocets or exercised missile firings on its guided-missile frigate, and its air search radar was removed in 1998. The ability to use the ship effectively in combat against a force equipped with modern sensors and countermeasures was uncertain, as was its ability to operate effectively with other ships in fleet operations.

The navy had four Lazaga-class 425-ton fast attack craft, all of which were equipped with four MM-38 Exocets and one 76-mm gun. The missile ships were generally considerably better manned and equipped than Morocco's other vessels. Individual officer training for these ships ranged from adequate to good, and crew training ranged from mediocre to adequate. These ships dated back to the early 1980s. One had its 76-mm gun removed in 1998.

Morocco had six 425-ton Cormoran-class large patrol craft with 40-mm and 20-mm guns. In the mid to late 1990s, the navy also commissioned five French-made, 580-ton Rais Bargach-class patrol craft with 20-mm and 40-mm guns and surface search radars. It had four 475-ton El Hahiq (Osprey 55-class) large patrol craft with one 40-mm and two 20-mm guns each. These were equipped with surface search radars and were commissioned in the late 1980s and 1990. Two of them were assigned to the customs service.

The Moroccan Navy had two Okba-class 445-ton large patrol craft with surface search radars and one 76-mm gun each. It also had six 100-ton El Wacil-class coastal/inshore patrol craft with 20-mm guns and surface search radars. The training and crew proficiency of these ships was suited largely for commercial patrol purposes.

The navy had one Newport-class landing ship tank (LST), displacing 8,450 tons fully loaded and with the capacity to carry 400 troops, 500 tons of vehicles, 3 landing craft for vehicles and personnel, and one large personnel landing craft. The ship has experienced repeated maintenance and operating problems. The navy also had three 1,409-ton Batral-class LSTs, which could carry 140 troops and 12 vehicles or 300 tons of cargo, and one Edic-class 670-ton landing craft (tank) that could carry up to 11 vehicles. Support craft include two small 1,500-ton transports and one Ro-Ro ferry converted to be a troop transport ship.

The customs service and coast guard have four P-32 coastal patrol craft, 18 Arcor-class coastal patrol craft, seven search and rescue (SAR) craft, and 15 Arcor 53-class inshore patrol craft.

The Moroccan Navy has shown that it can operate these fast attack craft, patrol craft, and transport and amphibious ships reasonably well. Yet, Morocco has limited repair and at-sea replenishment capability and most of its ships have limited endurance despite the use of two logistics support ships. Morocco has poor "blue water" capabilities, with the navy being capable of patrolling local waters and providing coastal defense but having only limited ability to operate in the Atlantic. Its capabilities for anti-air and anti-ship missile warfare are limited, and overall combat readiness training is said to be mediocre. Morocco would not be capable of successfully engaging Spanish naval forces with its current mix of naval assets and would experience serious problems in any engagement with Algeria.

On February 8, 2008, Dutch firm Schelde Naval Shipbuilding secured a contract with the Moroccan Navy for the construction of three SIGMA-class corvettes, one of which is to be the larger 105-m variant while the remaining two are to be smaller at 98 m, with delivery estimated for 2011–2012. The ships are likely to be armed with a single Oto Melara 76/62 gun, four MBDA MM-40 Exocet surface-to-surface missiles, and an MBDA vertical-launched MICA point-defense system.[6] The three ships will also be equipped with the TACTICOS combat management system, SMART-S Mk2 surveillance radar, a LIKOD

Mk2 tracking radar, a KINGKLIP hull-mounted sonar, along with an identification friend or foe (IFF) system and an electronic support and countermeasure suit.[7]

On April 18, 2008, Morocco finalized a deal to acquire a FREMM multi-mission frigate from France. In addition, Morocco decided to acquire three SIGMA corvettes. Slated for delivery in 2012–2013, the new 5,800-ton class of vessels is meant to boost France and Italy's naval antisubmarine, anti-surface, anti-air, and land-strike capabilities, and there will be versions of the vessels to meet all these roles.[8] Valued at $750 million, Morocco's commitment to acquire a FREMM-based frigate from France coincided with Rabat's decision to go ahead with an F-16 purchase from the United States instead of the French Rafale.[9]

Despite its limited defense budget, the Moroccan Navy has taken non-negligible steps to address its blue-water limitations. The acquisition of three SIGMA-class corvettes and one FREMM-class frigate would double Morocco's fleet of major missile-armed naval assets by 2013, not taking into account a sizeable increase in overall major ship quality.

MOROCCAN AIR FORCE

In 2008, the 13,000-man Moroccan Air Force had 89 combat-capable aircraft and 19 attack helicopters. There were major air bases in Kenitra, Marrakesh-Menara, Meknes-Mezergues, Rabat-Sale, and Sidi Slimane, as well as 3–4 operating bases in the south.

Morocco's forces included one fighter ground-attack squadron consisting of eight F-5As, two F-5Bs, 20 F-5Es, three F-5Fs, and 14 Mirage F-1EHs, plus one air defense squadron with 19 Mirage F-1CHs. It also had a reconnaissance squadron with four OV-10s and two CH-130s with side-looking radar as well as two C-130 and two Falcon 20 electronic intelligence and warfare planes. It had 51 training aircraft, including 19 Alphajets with dual capability in light attack missions.[10]

Morocco had relatively modern air munitions, including some AIM-9B/D/J Sidewinders, R-530s, R-550 Magics air-to-air missiles, as well as AGM-62B Walleye and AGM-65B Maverick air-to-surface missiles for its F-5Es. All of its combat aircraft are aging, however, and Moroccan efforts to fund more modern fighters will be discussed later.

Its relatively large transport forces included 15 C-130Hs, six CN-235s, two Do-28s, and two Falcon 20s, plus one Falcon 50, two Gulfstreams, four King Air 100s, and five Super King Air 200s. Morocco is one of the few air forces with tanker and mid-air refueling assets; it has one B-707 and two KC-130H transport/tanker aircraft. Morocco makes extensive use of air transport and supply in its operations against the Polisario.

Morocco had 19 SA-342 armed helicopters, seven armed with HOT ATGMs and 12 armed with cannons. These armed helicopters do not have advanced sensors and avionics, but are adequate for day combat. In late 2007, Morocco was expected to a sign a letter of intent to acquire 12 Eurocopter EC-725 combat search and rescue helicopters for its special forces, but it remains to be seen whether the sale will take place in the near future.[11] Morocco also has eight CH-47 heavy transport helicopters, 24 medium transport helicopters, and 41 light helicopters. Helicopter mobility and readiness are good by regional standards.

In addition, the air force uses its reconnaissance aircraft effectively, and its CH-130s with side-looking radar have proven to be of considerable value in monitoring the defensive wall in Western Sahara and in locating and targeting Polisario movements with vehicles. It seems able to make good use of its two C-130s and two Falcon 20 ELINT aircraft, and is one of the few regional air forces with such an electronic intelligence capability. It acquired a Westinghouse air defense system in the early 1980s, and has moderately effective warning and combat air control capability.

The Moroccan Air Force is one of the few regional air forces without a major land-based air defense component. Morocco has no medium or heavy SAM units and does not have the radar and battle management systems to support them. It has, however, upgraded its existing Northrop Grumman tactical radar system (TPS-63) with solid-state transmitters and digital signal processors (AN/TPS-63). This upgrade increases detection range by 250 percent and improves reliability, maintainability, and supportability. The air force has reasonably good warning and air control capability, but no airborne air control and warning assets and only limited surveillance and electronic warfare (EW) capabilities.

The Moroccan Air Force experienced considerable political instability in the early 1970s, and then faced significant challenges during the war with the Polisario. It lost a considerable number of aircraft to Polisario SA-6s and SA-7s in the early and mid-1980s, and often aborted missions or dropped bombs in locations where they had limited effect. Since that time, however, it has gradually corrected many of its past training, maintenance, and leadership problems. It has achieved a reasonable level of proficiency in using its Mirage F-1s, F-5E/Fs, and Alphajets in basic attack and support missions.

Although its 10 F-5A/Bs and 23 F-5E/Fs are adequate for missions against the Polisario, they are badly aged and lack modern avionics. They are not adequate for engaging modern fighters with beyond visual range radars and air-to-air missiles, and lack the avionics and sensors to use modern air-to-surface guided weapons at long ranges.

The air force also cannot properly operate all of its Mirage F-1 fighters, which constitute 33 aircraft out of its total combat strength of 89 aircraft. As previously mentioned, there are 14 Mirage F-1EHs in the attack role and 19 Mirage F-1CHs assigned to the air defense role. As of 2005, it was believed that more than one-half of Morocco's F-1s were grounded. It is unclear whether Morocco's problems in operating the Mirage F-1 stem from problems in maintaining the aircraft. In September 2005, France was awarded a $420 million contract to upgrade the aging fighters. Work on the upgrade, being carried out by French firms Sagem Defense Securite and Thales Airborne Systems, started in 2006 and covers 27 of Morocco's F-1CH/EHs.

The ASTRAC upgrade package included a new glass cockpit with a HOTAS control configuration fitted for night-vision goggle compatibility, new avionics, airframe modifications, Atar 9K-50 turbojet upgrades, new primary sensors in the form of the Thales RC400 multimode radar (similar to the Mirage 2000-5), new onboard computers, and laser gyro/GPS navigation equipment. The F-1s' upgraded combat capabilities will include MATRA MICA and Magic 2 air-to-air missiles, AM39 Exocet air-to-surface missiles, the new SAGEM AASM precision-guided munitions, laser-guided weapons capability, and a Thales Damocles targeting pod. The upgrade will also incorporate improved defensive capabilities, including a new radar warning system, jammer, and decoy dispensers. The upgrades are expected to give Morocco's F-1s full operational capabilities to meet expected future air-to-air and air-to-surface combat threats.[12]

Morocco will further augment its air-to-air and air-to-surface capabilities by acquiring 24 F-16C/D Block 50/52 fighter aircraft. France was initially expected to provide Morocco with a squadron of 18 of the next-generation Rafale fighter in a $3.1 billion deal. The $2.4 billion FMS includes 24 aircraft, engines, spare parts, spare APG-68(V)9 radar sets, countermeasure systems, radar warning receivers, the Joint Helmet Mounted Cueing System, SINCGAR radios, conformal fuel tanks, GPS and GPS/inertial navigation systems (INS), AN/AAQ-33/28 targeting pods, TARS (Recce [Reconnaissance]) pods, advanced IFF, EW suites, and a unit trainer.[13] In a last-minute addition, four Goodrich DB-110 Recce systems will also be included in the sale. These systems allow high-resolution imaging in both day and night conditions using visible-light and infrared sensors. The system has an effective operational range of 70 nautical miles and can be used to transmit real-time data to support tactical operations, battle-damage assessments, and alternate target selection.[14]

Morocco's air-to-air and air-to-surface munitions were also slated to be upgraded and augmented to match the F-16 purchase. The DSCA reported to Congress that Morocco requested an FMS that included the following:[15]

- 30 AIM-120C-5 AMRAAM air-to-air missiles

- 60 AIM-9M Sidewinder air-to-air missiles

- 20 HARM anti-radiation/radar missiles

- 8 AGM-65D/G Maverick air-to-surface missiles

- 45 AGM-65H Maverick air-to-surface missiles

- 50 JDAM tail kits, including 20 GBU-31s for Mk-82 500-lb bombs and 30 GBU-38s for Mk-84 2,000-lb bombs

- 20 GBU-24 Paveway III kits

- 50 GBU-10 Paveway II kits

- 150 GBU-12 Paveway II kits

- 60 Enhanced GBU-12 Paveway II bombs

- 300 Mk-82 training bombs

- 60,000 20-mm training projectiles

- 4,000 ALE-47 self-protection chaff and equipment

- 4,000 ALE-47 self-protection flares and equipment

The FMS was estimated to be as high as $155 million. Coupled with F-16s, the sale would not only give Morocco's air force significant capabilities in terms of air-to-air and air-to-surface targeting, tracking, and precision attack but would also provide Morocco with non-negligible anti-radar capabilities in the form of the HARM anti-radiation missile—a capability that Algeria and Tunisia did not possess in 2008, while Libya's anti-radiation missiles are older or obsolescent systems.

The air force also lacks advanced combat training capability. Morocco plans to acquire as many as 24 T-6B Texan training aircraft and supporting equipment and electronics, including GPS/INS from the United States. The FMS may cost as much $200 million. The T-6B is expected to supplement or replace the air force's existing T-37 trainers, which are high maintenance, exhibit high fuel consumption, and have low mission rates. The T-6Bs are expected to reduce Moroccan fuel requirements for training by as much as 66 percent.[16] Yet, this acquisition does not address Morocco's continuing maintenance problems and heavy dependence on foreign technicians

Morocco continues to have limited C^4I battle management capability in the event of a major Algerian attack. Some of these problems may be solved over the next few years as a result of Morocco's significant recent efforts to address its air combat and combat management weaknesses and through the continued acquisition of modern air combat systems.

MOROCCAN PARAMILITARY AND SECURITY FORCES

Like all Maghreb states, Morocco's military, paramilitary, and security forces play a major role in internal security and in safeguarding the power of the regime. Morocco's paramilitary forces total roughly 50,000 men, most of which can act as land forces. These include 20,000 men in the Gendarmerie Royale, which is organized into a coast-guard unit, a paratrooper squadron, a paramilitary brigade with four mobile groups, and one air squadron. The gendarmerie has 18 patrol boats, 2 light aircraft, and 22 helicopters.

The Border Police, the National Security Police, and the Judicial Police are departments of the Ministry of Interior, whereas the Royal Gendarmerie reports directly to the palace. Its activities are focused primarily on Islamic extremists, student and labor unrest, and the Sahrawis in Western Sahara.

Until recently, the Moroccan security apparatus has been repressive, and the security services have often acted as a power in their own right as well as a key source of support for the monarchy. The Ministry of Interior, which commands several overlapping police and paramilitary organizations, has controlled the rule of the security forces, or *makhzen*. The ministry has also exerted power through the fact that it determines eligibility for some aspects of welfare and free medical care and supervises the state and public committees dealing with investment and businesses in Morocco's 16 provinces.

The Ministry of Interior has been responsible for the conduct of elections, cooperation with the United Nations in the referendum on Western Sahara, the appointment and training of many local officials, the allocation of local and regional budgets, the oversight of university campuses, and the licensing of associations and political parties. The ministry has also exerted substantial influence over the judicial system.

NOTES

1. Data and information in the following section draws on interviews and details provided in the International Institute for Strategic Studies (IISS), *The Military Balance 2008*, http://www.iiss.org/publications/military-balance/the -military-balance-2008/.

2. Defense Security Cooperation Agency (DSCA), "Morocco – M109A5 155-mm Self-Propelled Howitzers," August 3, 2007, http://www.dsca.mil/ PressReleases/36-b/2007/Morocco_07-45.pdf (news release).

3. "Morocco Orders Tunguska-M1," *Jane's Missiles and Rockets*, April 1, 2005.

4. Tim Fish, "Morocco Plans Second Mediterranean Naval Base," *Jane's Navy International*, March 27, 2008; Lauren Gelfand, "Morocco Signs Up for NATO Counterinsurgency Operation," *Jane's Defense Weekly*, June 6, 2008.

5. This discussion draws heavily on interviews and the details provided in Stephen Saunders, ed., *Jane's Fighting Ships 2007–2008* (Jane's Information Group, 2007), and the country section in IISS, *The Military Balance*, 2008.

6. Richard Scott, "Morocco Confirms Order for SIGMA Frigates," *Jane's Defense Industry*, March 1, 2008.

7. Tim Fish, "Thales to Provide Systems for Morocco's SIGMA Frigates," *Jane's Navy International*, April 3, 2008.

8. Denise Hammick, "DCNS Finalizes Deal to Build FREMM Frigate for Morocco," *Jane's Defense Weekly*, April 23, 2008.

9. Peter Lewis, "Morocco Becomes First FREMM Export Customer," *Jane's Defense Weekly*, October 31, 2007.

10. This discussion draws heavily on the country section in IISS, *The Military Balance*, 2008.

11. J.A.C. Lewis, "Morocco Nears EC 725 Deal with Eurocopter," *Jane's Defense Industry*, October 11, 2007.

12. Jamie Hunter, "ASTRAC Upgrades Moroccan Mirages," *International Defense Review*, July 4, 2007.

13. Defense Security Cooperation Agency, "Morocco – F-16C/D Block 50/52 Aircraft," December 18, 2007, http://www.dsca.mil/PressReleases/36-b/2007/Morocco_08-20.pdf (news release).

14. Michael J. Gething, "Morocco Orders F-16 Recce Pods," *International Defense Review*, July 24, 2008.

15. DSCA, "Morocco – Weapons and Related Support for F-16 Aircraft," July 11, 2008, http://www.dsca.mil/PressReleases/36-b/2008/Morocco_08-37.pdf (news release).

16. Keri Smith, "U.S. Plans to Sell T-6B Trainers to Morocco," *Jane's Defense Industry*, December 20, 2007.

Figure 2.1 Moroccan Force Trends, 1985–2008

Category/Weapon	1985	1990	1995	2000	2002	2004	2005	2006	2007	2008
DEFENSE BUDGET (US$2008 billions)	0.504	1.36	1.23	1.8	1.5	2.0	2.07	2.16	2.47	-
MOBILIZATION BASE										
Men Ages 13–17 (in thousands)	-	1,437	1,600	1,690	1,780	1,780	-	-	-	-
Men Ages 18–22 (in thousands)	-	1,343	1,439	1,526	1,612	1,612	-	-	-	-
MANPOWER										
Active	149,000	192,500	195,500	196,300	198,500	196,300	196,300	200,800	200,800	195,800
(Conscripts)	-	-	100,000	100,000	100,000	100,000	100,000	100,000	100,000	100,000
Reserve	-	100,000	150,000	-	150,000	150,000	150,000	150,000	150,000	150,000
Total	149,000	292,500	249,500	196,300	348,500	346,300	346,300	350,800	350,800	345,800
Paramilitary	33,000	40,000	42,000	42,000	48,000	50,000	50,000	50,000	50,000	50,000
LAND FORCES										
Active Manpower	130,000	175,000	175,000	175,000	175,000	175,000	175,000	175,000	180,000	175,000
(Conscripts)	-	-	100,000	100,000	100,000	100,000	100,000	100,000	100,000	100,000
Reserve Manpower	-	-	150,000	-	150,000	150,000	150,000	150,000	150,000	150,000
Total Manpower	130,000	175,000	325,000	175,000	325,000	325,000	325,000	325,000	330,000	325,000
Main Battle Tanks	190	284	524	524	744	520	520	540	540	380(200)
AIFVs/Arm. Cars/Lt. Tanks	612	474	559	559	539	215	215	186	186	186
APCs/Recces/Scouts	806	879	785	785	1,109	1,064	1,064	1,149	1,149	1,149
ATGM Launchers	-	850	720	720	720	720	720	790	790	790

(continued)

Figure 2.1 *(continued)*

Category/Weapon	1985	1990	1995	2000	2002	2004	2005	2006	2007	2008
SP Artillery/Anti-tank Guns	174?	230	175	167	227	227	227	199	199	199
Towed Artillery	174	144	164	190	185	185	185	118	118	118
MRLs	20	40	39	39	26	40	40	35	35	35
Mortars	1,290	680+	1,700	1,700	1,470	1,470	1,470	2,540	2,540	1,706
SSM Launchers	-	-	-	0	0	0	0	0	0	0
AA Guns	140	427	-	425	425	425	460	457	457	407
Lt. SAM Launchers	-	-	107	107	107	107	107	107	107	107
AIR & AIR DEFENSE FORCES										
Active Manpower	13,000	13,500	13,500	13,500	13,500	13,500	13,500	13,000	13,000	13,000
Reserve Manpower	-	-	-	-	-	-	-	-	-	-
Aircraft										
Total Fighters/FGA/Recces	105	93	99	89	74	95	95	72	72	72
Bombers	0	0	0	0	0	0	0	0	0	0
Fighters	0	15	15	15	15	15	15	19	19	19
FGA	77	31	34	47	53	54	54	47	47	47
Recces	0	6	2	6	6	6	6	6	6	6
COIN/OCU	28	46	50	0	0	0	0	0	0	0
Airborne Early Warning (AEW)	0	0	0	0	0	0	0	0	0	0
Electronic Warfare (EW)	0	3	3	3	3	4	4	4	4	4
Maritime Reconnaissance	0	0	0	0	0	0	0	0	0	0
Combat-Capable Trainers	52	-	12	23	23	24	24	19	19	19
Tankers	0	4	3	3	3	3	3	3	3	3
Transport	33	33	35	36	33	33	33	44	44	44

(continued)

Figure 2.1 *(continued)*

Category/Weapon	1985	1990	1995	2000	2002	2004	2005	2006	2007	2008
Helicopters										
Attack/Armed/ASW	18	50	24	24	24	24	24	19	19	19
Other	90	24	89	88	89	88	88	73	73	73
Total	108	74	113	112	113	112	112	92	92	92
SAM Forces										
Batteries	0	0	0	0	0	0	0	0	0	0
Heavy Launchers	0	0	0	0	0	0	0	0	0	0
NAVAL FORCES										
Active Manpower	6,000	7,000	7,000	7,800	10,000	7,800	7,800	7,800	7,800	7,800
Reserve Manpower	-	-	-	-	-	-	-	-	-	-
Total Manpower	6,000	7,000	7,000	7,800	10,000	7,800	7,800	7,800	7,800	7,800
Submarines	0	0	0	0	0	0	0	0	0	0
Destroyers/Frigates/Corvettes	1	1	3	1	1	2	2	3	3	3
Missile	1	1	3	1	1	2	2	3	3	3
Other	0	0	0	0	0	0	0	0	0	0
Missile Patrol	6	4	4	4	4	4	4	4	4	4
Coastal/Inshore Patrol	17	21	23	23	23	23	23	23	23	23
Mine	0	0	0	0	0	0	0	0	0	0
Amphibious Ships	4	3	4	4	4	4	4	4	4	4
Landing Craft/Light Support	-	-	-	8	8	8	8	8	8	8
ASW/Combat Helicopters	-	-	-	0	0	2	2	3	3	3

Source: Adapted by Anthony H. Cordesman from data provided by U.S. experts, and from the International Institute for Strategic Studies, *The Military Balance*, various editions.

Note: Figures in parentheses are additional equipment in storage or not operational. SSM launchers are major systems. "O" connotes that a zero number has been verified, whereas "-" connotes that data are not known or verifiable.

3

THE MILITARY FORCES OF ALGERIA

Algeria's military developments have been dominated by a corrupt and inefficient military junta, sometimes called "The Power," which rules the country behind the façade of an elected government. The military has lost some of its political power in recent years, and its leadership has improved somewhat. It remains a major factor in Algerian politics, however, and its behavior is often shaped more by political considerations and internal security concerns than by a focus on national defense and military effectiveness.

From the early 1990s to 2002, Algeria was engaged in a violent civil war with Islamic extremists after more moderate Islamic political factions were denied power following their victory in a popular election. The civil war was vicious on both sides, often involving large-scale atrocities. Although the government and the armed forces largely won the conflict by 2002, sporadic violence and minor skirmishes have continued to take place.

The government in Algiers was successful in suppressing the Islamist threat throughout 2005 and much of 2006, but this changed in 2007 when the largest surviving Islamist militia, the Salafist Group for Preaching and Combat (GPSC), reoriented and rebranded itself along lines mimicking Abu Musab al-Zarqawi's al Qaeda in Iraq (AQIA). Now calling itself al Qaeda in the Islamic Maghreb (AQIM), the group poses a significant national security threat to Algeria, adopting AQIA-style multiple-suicide bombings as its weapon of choice.[1] The group has carried out a number of successful high-casualty operations in the country and also threatens to destabilize Algeria's neighbors by providing logistical and training support to similar—if underdeveloped—Islamist groups in Libya, Morocco, and Tunisia. Combating AQIM—and consequently solidifying the military's counterinsurgency and antiterrorism role—is one of the Algerian military's main priorities.

The trends in Algerian military forces are shown in **Figure 3.1**. Algeria has changed its force posture over time to reflect the state of its improving relations with Morocco, its declining perception of a threat from Libya, the country's economic problems, and its need to focus on post–civil war reconstruction and armed-forces development. Algerian regular military manpower peaked at around 170,000 in the mid-1980s, but declined to around 125,000 by 1990. It dropped to less than 122,000 in 1995, but has since increased slowly. Algeria had 147,000 actives as of 2008, including approximately 80,000 conscripts. It had an on-paper reserve strength of some 150,000, with little or no real-world readiness or war-fighting capability.

Algeria's civil war led the country to expand its paramilitary forces from around 30,000 men in 1985 to about 187,200 in 2008, with 20,000 in the army-controlled gendarmerie, 16,000 in the Directorate of National Security Forces, 1,200 in the Republican Guard, and around 150,000 in the Legitimate Defense Groups. To compare these figures to those of the different Islamist groups, the peak threat consisted of only 2,000–3,000 full-time regulars in the Group Islamique Armee (GIA), operating in small groups of 50–100. The Armed Front for Islamic Jihad (FIDA) and Islamic League for the Call and Jihad (LIDD) probably peaked at less than 1,000 actives each during the civil war, and AQIM/GPSC was said to have as many as 800 fighters in 2006.[2] There is no way, however, to quantify the numbers of sympathizers or part-time fighters.

Algeria has a fairly large pool of major weapons systems. Its military forces have 895 MBTs, 90 armored reconnaissance vehicles, 1,040 AIFVs, 750 APCs, 170 SP artillery, 375 towed artillery, and 144 MRLs. Its air force possesses 141 combat aircraft and 33 attack helicopters. Its naval forces have two submarines, nine major surface ships, 20 patrol craft, and three amphibious ships.

The Algerian military will receive a number of major land, air, sea, and C⁴I systems over next few years, and acquisitions are set to continue through 2010–2013. Russia is Algeria's largest arms and systems supplier, with a March 2006 deal outlining Russian defense exports to Algeria worth $7.5 billion and the cancellations of Algeria's debts to the former Soviet Union, which are estimated at $4.5 billion. The deal will revitalize Algeria's aging fleet of MBTs, AIFVs, multi-role combat aircraft, and major SAM systems.[3]

Aside from its ongoing Russian acquisitions, Algeria has also placed offers to acquire combat systems from European suppliers. The navy hopes to acquire variants of the French FREMM multi-role frigate—an effort mirroring Morocco's effort to upgrade its naval asset pool—and Italian firm SELEX Sistemi Integrati will upgrade Algeria's C⁴I capabilities.[4]

Although these sales do not directly address manpower, training, and communications integration weaknesses, Algeria's major drive for new acquisitions and the trade-in or replacement of aging and obsolescent systems is significant both for Algeria and for the regional military balance.

ALGERIAN ARMY

Algeria's military forces are known as the National Popular Army (ANP). The Algerian Army is by far the largest element of the ANP and is currently organized into six military regions while plans to reorganize the force into a division structure remain on hold. Like Libya and Morocco, Algeria has gradually built up a network of roads and facilities in its border areas that are designed to allow its forces to deploy and fight against either neighbor. Many of its units are not deployed in the border area, however, and the Algerian Army is scarcely on a wartime footing. The army has major bases at Algiers, Annaba, Batna, Becher, Biskra, Blida, Constantine, Djanet, El Golea, Ghardaia, In Salah, Oran, Ouargla, Reggane, Skikda, Tamanrasset, Tarat, Timimoun, Tindouf, and Touggourt.

At the top of the chain of command is the Higher Council of State to the General Staff, headed by the president as commander in chief. The army is in turn led by the chief of staff of the ANP, followed by the commander of the land forces, the commanders of the six military regions, and the commander of the joint military academy. The chief of staff has a separate inspector general and exercises a direct line of command to the army's major combat units. The organization of the army has been streamlined since 1996, but still has a highly bureaucratic and grossly overmanned and overranked headquarters and support structure. It would probably be more efficient with one-third less manpower.

In the mid-1980s, the army reorganized its divisions into something approaching a modern regimental structure, added armored forces, and attempted to modernize its command structure. The army is now organized into two armored divisions, each including three tank regiments and one mechanized infantry regiment. The army has one airborne division with five airborne regiments, six antiaircraft defense battalions, and 20 independent infantry battalions. Depending on the source, it has 2–7 artillery battalions and 5–7 air defense battalions, one of which is a SAM unit. Most of these latter battalions are part of, and act in support of, a given division and its force structure.[5]

Algeria also has large paramilitary forces, which carried out most of the fighting in the civil war. The Ministry of the Interior has the 16,000-man National Security Force, which is used as an antiterrorist and security force in desert and mountain areas. The Republican Guard Brigade is a 1,200-man force with armored reconnaissance vehicles that aids in border surveillance and antiterrorist operations in desert areas. A 50,000-man police force and a 20,000-man gendarmerie controlled by the Ministry of Defense are used for security and antiterrorism as well as policing.

As of 2008, the regular army had about 47,000 full-time actives and 80,000 conscripts, adding up to a total force of some 127,000 men. Conscripts serve for 18 months, of which six months involves basic training and the remaining 12 encompass various civil projects. Algerian conscripts generally receive inadequate basic unit and field training. Algeria also has a large army reserve of 150,000 on paper, but it has little real structure and only limited and highly selective call-up training. It would take weeks to retrain most reserves to serve basic military functions and months to create effective reserve units.

The Algerian Army had roughly 895 tanks, including 270 T-54/55s, 300 T-62s, and 325 T-72s, 55 of which were delivered during the 1999–2000 period. It had 90 BDRM-2 reconnaissance vehicles (64 with AT-3 Saggers), and possibly 49 Saladins. It had 1,040 AIFVs, including 680 BMP-1s and 260 BMP-2s. Continuing deliveries of BMP-2s took place during 1999 and 2000. It had some 750 APCs, including 100 TH 390 Fahds, 300 BTR-60/OT-64s, 150 BTR-80s, 150 OT-64s and 50 M-3 Panhards. The overall readiness of Algerian armor was limited by significant obsolescence and maintenance problems; little large-unit training; and poor to mediocre training in rapid maneuver, night warfare, support and logistics, and aggressive offensive combat.

As part of the 2006 arms deal, Russia was expected to equip Algeria with at least 40 modern T-90S MBTs, but *Jane's Defense Weekly* reported in 2008 that as many as 180 T-90s may be delivered. It is unclear whether shipment of new units is under way and whether the 2011 deadline set in 2006 will be met. The emphasis now seems to be on an initial delivery of new equipment in addition to upgrade kits for Algeria's current fleet of 325 T-72s.[6]

Algeria will also be upgrading its fleet of BMP-2s to the BMP-2M standard. The BMP-2M will have automatic day and night fire-control systems with automatic tracking and an armament suite that includes four 9M 133 Kornet-E ATGMs, a 2A42 30-mm canon, and a 7.62-mm machine gun. The addition of the Kornet-E will allow upgraded BMP-2s to defeat 1,000–1,200-mm armor using either a hollow-charge or thermobaric warhead from an effective range of 5.5 km. The 2A42 cannon can field either armor-piercing or high-explosive rounds from up to 2.2 or 1.6 km, respectively. The combination of tracking, ATGMs, and improved targeting would give the BMP-2M added flexibility and the ability to take on tasks usually given to heavier units and MBTs.[7]

In 2008, the army had 375 major towed artillery weapons, including 160 D-30, 25 D-74, 100 M-1931/37, and 60 M-1938 122-mm weapons; 10 M-46 130-mm weapons; and 20 ML-20 M-1937 152-mm weapons. It also had 170 SP artillery weapons, including 140 122-mm 2S1s and 30 2S3 152-mm weapons. Its MRL strength included 48 122-mm BM-21s, 48 140-mm BM-14s and BM-16s, 30 BM-24 240-mm weapons, and 18 newer long-range Smerch 9A52s. It had 150 82-mm, 120 120-mm, and 60 160-mm mortars. This artillery strength included far more SP weapons than Algeria had in the mid-1980s, and the army has moderate capabilities for mass fire against static or area targets. It has little training in artillery maneuver, however, and poor capabilities for combined arms, counterbattery fire, switching fire, and beyond visual range targeting.

The Algerian Army had 160 ZIS-2 M-1943 towed 57-mm and 80 D-44 85-mm anti-tank guns, plus 10 T-12 and 50 Su-100 100-mm SP weapons in storage. The 57-mm weapons are obsolete, and the 85-mm D-44s are obsolescent, having limited anti-armor capability against modern tanks. Other anti-tank weapons include approximately 200 Milans, AT-3 Saggers, and the newer AT-4 Spigot and AT-5 Spandrel anti-tank guided weapons (ATGWs). As previously mentioned, some of the Saggers are mounted on BRDM-2s. The army also had 180 recoilless rifles. Few crews have realistic combat training in killing tanks or other armor.

The army had about 875 air defense guns, including 225 SP radar-guided ZSU-23-4s. It also had more than 220 man-portable SA-7s, SA-14s, and SA-16s, along with 48 SA-8 and 20 SA-9 light SP SAM launchers. Although most of its air defense weapons have limited lethality and most crews have limited training, Algeria has enough modern weapons and sheer weapons strength to provide a considerable "curtain fire" capability against low-flying aircraft.

These weapons holdings show that Algeria has adequate numbers of weapons for a 127,000-man army. Yet, much of Algeria's equipment is 10–20 years old, and some is no longer fully operational. This includes many BTR combat vehicles and some towed artillery weapons. Algeria needs more SP artillery weapons, more modern short-range air defenses, and far more third- and fourth-generation ATGMs. It also needs modern artillery counterbattery radars and fire-control equipment and improved command, control, and communications systems. It would have to be extensively re-equipped for effective night combat and beyond visual range targeting.

The Algerian Army has had no meaningful combat experience against a regular army since its border clashes with Morocco in 1963. The army is heavily politicized, corrupt, and nepotistic, which affects promotion at the higher levels of command. It spends far more time on internal security problems than on developing its war-fighting capability.

Training tends to be overly rigid and repetitive. Combined arms, combined operations, and maneuver training are poor. Leadership is weak at every level, and corruption in the ranks only adds to serious organizational, training, logistical, and combat and service support problems. Technical training and maintenance standards are low. The army often buys new equipment more quickly than it can effectively absorb it, and then fails to follow up with effective training, maintenance, and logistics subsystems.

The army's military culture is slowly modernizing, but it retains an awkward mix of Algerian ideology and long-outdated and relatively slow-moving Soviet tactics and doctrine. The army has traditionally relied on mass and attrition rather than on maneuver and technology.

Its leadership has never fully converted from an ideological focus on the army as a popular or revolutionary force to one that is fully capable of modern armored and maneuver combat. Algeria's internal security problems and the high degree of politicization and bureaucratization of its forces have made it difficult to change this situation. Yet, closer ties with French and U.S. advisors since the 1990s have contributed to a more flexible military doctrine, especially given the army's growing role in counterinsurgency, rapid deployment, and patrol and exercise operations with NATO.

Strikingly, it is the paramilitary forces and militias that have done so much of the actual fighting in the Algerian civil war, rather than the regular army, which constituted an immense drain on national resources for so many years. The Algerian National Security Force, Republican Guard Brigade, police force, and gendarmerie performed most security antiterrorism functions during the civil war years. Much of the responsibility for security has also been turned over to the extensive regional militia forces and the Legitimate Defense Groups. Whereas Morocco painfully learned how to fight a guerrilla war, the Algerian Army largely stood aside and let proxies do much of the fighting.

The relatively small size of the organized military forces of the Islamic opposition during the war is also striking. The GIA is estimated to have had small groups of 50–100 men, totaling less than 3,000 actives. The FIDA is estimated to have had small groups of 50–100 men; no estimate of total active strength is available. The same is true of LIDD.[8]

Although the civil war may be largely over, an Islamist extremist terrorist threat remains and could potentially grow back to the level of an insurgency if Algeria's government does not move forward with economic development, jobs for its young men, and reform. Algeria will still need C[4]I capabilities to better coordinate threat analyses, emergency and human resource management, and overall support to the communication of major command decisions. Algeria announced in early 2008 that it will be expanding on the initial phase and coverage of the county's United Information and Telecommunications Network Project (RUNITEL 1). Whereas RUNITEL 1 added coverage, capacity, and C[4]I capabilities mainly to the capital Algiers, the next phase, RUNITEL 2, to be implemented by Italian firm SELEX Sistemi Integrati, will mainly cover Algeria's resource-rich southern regions.[9]

The recent escalation of violence between AQIM and the central government have increasingly put the spotlight on the army and the gendarmerie as they continue to develop their counterinsurgency and counterterrorism capabilities against an organization that has adopted AQIA-style multiple-suicide operations as its tactic of choice. This tactic was used only once during the entirety of the civil war and killed numerous Algerian bystanders, whose support AQIM needs to swell their ranks. AQIM is running the risk of further alienating Algerians who are already exhausted and reticent at the prospect of yet another round of jihad at home.

ALGERIAN AIR FORCE

Algeria's air force had roughly 14,000 actives in 2008. It initially emerged as a modern force as the result of an expansion that took place in the mid-1970s after clashes between Algerian and Moroccan forces. It had 141 combat aircraft and 33 armed helicopters. The air force is organized along Soviet lines, although Pakistan provided advisors and pilots and Egypt provided air training. Its main missions are the defense of Algerian cities and conducting air defense and attack operations in the event of a conflict with Libya or Morocco. It has bases in central Algeria at Ain Oussera, Blida, Boufarik, and Bou Sfer; near the Moroccan border at Bechar/Oukda, Mecheira, Oran, and Tindouf; and near the Libyan border at Biskra. The air force also has dispersal bases at Ozukar and Sidid bei Abbas.

The combat strength of the Algerian Air Force is organized into regiments. As of 2008, it had five fighter ground-attack regiments, which include two with a total of 17 Su-24Ms, two with 38 MiG-23BNs, and one squadron of six newer Su-30MKAs. Algeria reportedly ordered 22 Su-24s from Russia in October 2000. Deliveries were to start in November 2000, and all were to be delivered and in service by late 2001. The Su-24s were to be the same Su-24M (Fencer D) model already in service in Algeria and were to be taken from Russia's operational inventory, with some upgrading and reconditioning.

The air force had five fighter regiments, one with 25 MiG-29C/UBs, and two with a total of 12 MiG-25s. The air force had two reconnaissance squadrons, one with four MiG-25Rs and one with four Su-24Es. Some reports indicate that Algeria also had four Su-24 MR (Fencer E) reconnaissance aircraft.[10]

With the exception of Algeria's 48 Su-30s, Su-24s, and MiG-29s— the latter two dating back to the 1980s while the former is a modern update of the Su-27—Algeria's 141 combat aircraft are now badly dated. The Su-30s, Su-24s, and MiG-29s are the only aircraft with modern avionics; the capability to fight effectively in night, all-weather, and beyond visual range air-to-air combat; or the ability to use air-to-ground ordnance with high effectiveness. Algeria's attack aircraft lack the avionics, sensors, all-weather navigation aids, and computers needed to take advantage of modern precision-guided weapons.

Algeria's six Su-30s are part of an initial delivery under the aforementioned $7.5 billion arms sale from Russia; Algeria will have a total force strength of 28 Su-30MKAs by 2010. The arms sale was not without incident, with Algeria returning a number of MiG-29s delivered in 2007 on the basis that the aircraft were substandard and secondhand rather than new. It was not clear as of mid-2008 if Algeria and Russia came to an agreement as to whether the delivery of 28 MiG-29MTs and six two-seat MiG-29UBTs would go ahead.[11]

There were two maritime reconnaissance squadrons with six Super King Air B-200Ts, but it is unclear whether all of these aircraft are operational. Algeria had a large number of training aircraft, some of which were part of its combat strength. They included six YAK-130s, 36 L-39Zs, seven L-39Cs, and 40 Z-142s. Algeria is slated to receive an additional 10 YAK-130s for a total of 16 aircraft, in addition to the suspended delivery of six MiG-29UBTs.

Algeria's receipt of additional modern aircraft is part of a broader effort to counteract serious long-term modernization problems. Many U.S. and French experts question the merit of past Algerian attempts to reconfigure its aging Soviet systems to use Western technology. These experts believe that re-engineering Soviet fighters and trying to upgrade Soviet electronics and avionics would raise the life-cycle cost of such equipment above the cost of new Russian or Western equipment.

Accordingly, the purchase of new equipment is ultimately the most practical and pragmatic option for the air force. In a departure from past sales and deliveries, Russia has offered to trade in Algeria's fleet of aging and obsolescent MiG-21s, MiG-23s, MiG-25s, and about 20 used MiG-29s that it had acquired from Belarus and Ukraine. The scheme is a one-for-one trade-in arrangement. It is noteworthy that Algeria no longer has MiG-21s—by far its oldest fighters—in service or in storage. At least in this case, Algeria has opted for new systems rather than costly upgrades.[12]

The air force possessed a total of 33 Mi-24 attack helicopters, organized into four squadrons. Algeria's Mi-24s are Superhind Mk IIIs, armed with Denel Kentron Ingwe laser-riding anti-armor missiles with a range of more than 5 km. These helicopters also have Thales's programmable chaff and flare dispensers. Russia has delivered six Mi-171 upgraded helicopters employing Geofizika night-vision technology, with 36 more to come.[13]

The air force had 114 transport helicopters, including eight AS-355 Ecureuil, 42 Mi-171s, and 64 Mi-17s in a support capacity. Algeria is also expected to receive six AW101 Merlins and four Super Lynx Series 300 during 2009–2010. The helicopters will be unarmed and used primarily for search and rescue (SAR) and maritime patrol operations.[14]

Algeria had an extensive supply of fixed-wing transport and VIP aircraft, including nine C-130Hs, eight C-130H-30s, nine IL-76MD/TDs, two L100-300s, three Falcon 900s, four Gulfstream IV-SPs, one Gulfstream V, and two F-27s.

Algeria's SAM forces are organized into three SAM regiments. As of 2008, there were an estimated 140–180 SA-2, SA-3, and SA-6 launchers and some 48 SA-8s. Algeria had three brigades of air defense artillery units with 725 unguided 85-mm, 100-mm, and 130-mm weapons.

The SA-2, SA-3, and SA-6 are aging systems that are vulnerable to a range of modern countermeasures. Algeria has purchased eight batteries of the very capable S-300PMU-2 heavy air defense system, as well as 24 Almaz-Antei 2S6M Tunguska 30-mm/SA-19 SP short-range air defense platforms.[15] It is not clear whether deliveries have commenced, and it will take some time before these new systems are integrated into the Algerian air defense framework and properly manned with adequately trained personnel. The Algerian air defense C⁴I, air defense and warning system, and radar sensor net's obsolescence and the absence of modern battle management and EW capability will further hamper the integration and use of new systems.

The air force has no real combat experience, and training is outdated and poorly organized for either large-scale attack or air defense operations. Reconnaissance, EW, and countermeasure capabilities range from poor to mediocre, and Algeria does not seem to have received the level of technical support or upgrading that the USSR provided to Libya. Maintenance standards are poor, and some aircraft are virtually in storage because of a lack of trained manpower and support capability.

The Algerian Air Force also suffers from limited and obsolescent C⁴I/battle management capability as well as serious problems in the quality and modernization of its air control and warning capabilities. Its SA-2, SA-3, SA-6, and SA-8 units and air defense brigades have low readiness and operational capability and poor aircraft and munitions operability and technology.

ALGERIAN NAVY

The 6,000-man Algerian Navy is based at Algiers (1st Region), Annaba (GG headquarters), Jijel (5th Region), and Mers el Kebir (2nd Region). It is under the command of a major general and headquartered at Algiers. In addition to the navy, Algeria has 500 men in its coast guard. The navy has a strength of two submarines, three frigates, six corvettes, nine missile fast attack craft, 11 fast attack coastal patrol craft, and three amphibious ships. The navy also has one survey ship, one major auxiliary ship, and several tug and support vessels. The coastal defense force has four truck-mounted batteries of SS-C-3 Styx coastal anti-ship defense missiles that are based at Algiers, Jijel, and Mers-el-Kebir and linked by coastal surveillance radars.[16]

The navy's two 2,325-ton Kilo-class (type 877E) submarines are equipped with six 533-mm torpedo tubes, long-range torpedoes with active/passive homing, and pattern active/passive homing torpedoes and mines. These submarines, originally refitted in 1995 and 1996, are active but still seem to have little operational training. One of the submarines is currently undergoing a second refit. Algeria used to have two additional Romeo-class submarines, but these left the fleet in 1989 and are now restricted to training. As a result, Algeria has sought to acquire up to two more Kilos. The purpose and mission of Algeria's submarine force is unclear. Its operating standards are as low as those of most navies of developing nations. Algeria could not use these submarines effectively against a modern Western navy, and it is unclear how they would be used against Libya or Morocco.

The Algerian Navy's major surface ships are more capable. The navy has three Mourad Rais class, 1,900-ton ASW frigates (ex-Soviet Koni-class), armed with four 76-mm and twin launcher SA-N-4 Gecko SAMs (with a maximum range of 15 km or 8 nautical miles and a speed of Mach 0.9). It also has two RBU 6000 Smerch 2 ASW rocket launchers, mine rails, and depth charges. The ships date back to the early to mid-1980s. The ships have relatively modern air-surface radars and fire-control systems, but they only have decoys and chaff launchers as countermeasures and do not have torpedo tubes. They are all active, but one ship is used for training purposes. One ship was refitted in Russia during 1997–2000 and has returned to service. A second ship is to be refitted but no date has been announced, and further modifications of these ships may be possible as part of the $7.5 billion Russian arms and upgrade package.

The navy has three 660-ton Rais Hamidou class missile corvettes (ex-Soviet Nanuchka-class) armed with SS-N-2Cs (active radar or IR homing to 46 km or 25 nautical miles) ship-to-ship missiles (SSMs), twin launcher SA-N-4 SAMs, and two 57-mm guns. These were delivered as new ships during 1980–1982. One completed a refit in 1998–2000, and a second is scheduled to be refitted, but no date has been announced.

There are also two 540-ton Chinese-designed Type 802 or Djebel Chenona-class coastal patrol corvettes, each armed with one 76-mm gun and two twin CSS-N-8 Saccade tactical SSMs. They lack effective fire-control systems, but do have surface search radars. The ships were delivered in 1985 and 1990, but the second ship ran into financing problems and is not fitted with a main gun. Neither seems fully combat operational.

The navy also has nine Osa II 210-245-ton missile fast attack craft plus three non-operational Osa I 210-ton attack craft. Each is armed with four SS-N-2B anti-ship missiles with infrared and radar homing. The SS-N-2B is an aging system vulnerable to countermeasures, but has a maximum speed of Mach 0.9 and range of 80 km (43 nautical miles) with semi-active radar or IR homing. These ships are rarely seen at sea, and it is unclear whether more than six Osa II-class craft and their weapons systems are fully operational. They were delivered in the late 1970s and early 1980s, and need refitting and re-engining.

Algeria has at least 11 active 200-ton Kebir-class (Brooke Marine) patrol boats with one 76-mm gun each, plus two twin 25-mm guns and two twin 14.5-mm guns, and the navy has ordered 15 more, although financing problems have delayed construction and delivery of the additional ships. Six have been transferred to the coast guard. These boats have surface search radars, but do not have modern countermeasures or serious aid defense capabilities.

The navy's amphibious strength is large enough to give Algeria the potential capability to conduct landings against Libya or Morocco. It has two British-made 2,450-ton LSTs (with a capacity of 240 troops, seven tanks, and one helicopter) and one 834-ton Polnochny B-class medium landing ship with a capacity of 180 troops and six tanks.

The navy also operates one survey ship, two support ships, a number of tugs, 15 fishery and coastal protection craft, and six Beechcraft Super Knight 200T aircraft with weather radars. These aircraft are only capable of visual reconnaissance. The 500-man coast guard, under the navy's command, has 29 small ships and two more under construction.

The Algerian Navy has reasonable ship strength and a number of modern combat surface ships that have considerable anti-ship missile capability by regional standards, and may have or be acquiring SS-N-25 missiles. Its air defense and countermeasure capabilities are more limited, however, and several of its ships are obsolescent and poorly equipped in terms of sensors and weaponry. The navy has poor operational performance, overall readiness, training, and equipment quality.

At its current force strength and quality, the navy could not defend itself adequately against Western strike aircraft or anti-ship missile attacks, but would probably be able to defeat either the Libyan or Moroccan navies. As previously mentioned, Algeria is currently negotiating to acquire four FREMM-class multi-role frigates from France.[17] Although the sale, estimated at some $594 million, has not been finalized as of mid-2008, these very modern ships would give the Algerian Navy a decisive force numbers and quality advantage over Libya, Morocco, or Tunisia.

ALGERIAN PARAMILITARY AND SECURITY FORCES

Some of the problems with Algeria's conventional war-fighting capabilities are explained by the fact that the internal threats that it faces are far more serious than its foreign ones. During its bitter civil war, the main function of the military and paramilitary forces was to fight rebel forces and maintain the power of the regime. No quarter was given on either side, and much of the government's internal security forces, including virtually all of the 150,000-man Legitimate Self-Defense Force, are little more than armed rabble. As of 2008 it remained a force of poorly trained and ill-organized local militias that carried out massacres and bloody reprisals during the war years.

The government's formal paramilitary forces and security apparatus are composed of the army, air force, navy, and national gendarmerie (the national police). The less formal elements include the communal guards (a local police) and local self-defense forces. The U.S. Department of State reports that all of these elements are involved in counterinsurgency and counterterrorism operations and are under the control of the government. All have been responsible for numerous serious human rights abuses.

One of the best-organized paramilitary forces is the 1,200-man Republican Guard, a small, elite security force armed with AML-60s and M-3s. Others include the gendarmerie, a force of 20,000 men assigned to the Ministry of Defense that has 44 AML-60 and 110 M-3 armored vehicles, 100 Fahd armored personnel carriers, and Mi-2 helicopters. It is reasonably well trained and organized along military lines, and has played a major role in the government's efforts to assert control over the Islamic Salvation Front and in its armed clashes with Islamic fundamentalists. The 16,000-man National Security Forces have mediocre training and are equipped mostly with small arms.

NOTES

   1. "Algeria's New Jihad," *Jane's Terrorism & Security Monitor*, May 10, 2007.
   2. Ibid.
   3. Robin Hughes, "Rosoboronexport Details Algerian T-90 Acquisition," *Jane's Defense Weekly*, July 13, 2008; Guy Anderson, "Russia Concludes USD 7.5 Billion Defense Export Deal with Algeria," *Jane's Defense Industry*, March 13, 2006.
   4. Luca Peruzzi, "SELEX Sistemi Integrati Wins Contract to Expand Algeria's RUNITEL," *International Defense Review*, January 18, 2008; J.A.C. Lewis, "Algeria Negotiates on FREMM Acquisition," *Jane's Defense Weekly*, February 22, 2008.
   5. This discussion draws heavily on interviews and the details provided in *Jane's World Armies*, various editions, and the country section in the International Institute for Strategic Studies (IISS), *The Military Balance*, 2008, p. 236.
   6. Robin Hughes, "Rosoboronexport Details Algerian T-90 Acquisition," *Jane's Defense Weekly*, July 13, 2008; Guy Anderson, "Russia Concludes USD 7.5 Billion Defense Export Deal with Algeria," *Jane's Defense Industry*, March 13, 2006.
   7. Nikolai Novichkov, "Defendory '06: Algeria Is First Foreign Customer for BMP-2M Upgrade," *Jane's Defense Weekly*, October 26, 2006.
   8. IISS, *The Military Balance*, various editions.
   9. Luca Peruzzi, "SELEX Sistemi Integrati Wins Contract to Expand Algeria's RUNITEL," *International Defense Review*, January 18, 2008.
   10. IISS, *The Military Balance*, various editions.

11. Lauren Gelfand, "Algeria Takes Delivery of Russian Fighters, Reviving Major Defense Deal," *Jane's Defense Weekly*, June 6, 2008; Vladimir Petrov, "Algeria Suspends Russian Arms Package," *Jane's Defense Weekly*, February 15, 2008.

12. This discussion draws heavily on details provided in Henry Ivanov, "Algeria and Russia to Sign USD 3 Billion Arms Deal," *Jane's Defense Weekly*, January 20, 2008; the country section in IISS, *The Military Balance*, 2008, p. 237.

13. "Algeria to Get Night-Upgraded Mi-171 Helicopters," *Jane's Defense Weekly*, January 15, 2003; "Mil Mi-24D Attack Helicopter Upgrade Package Undergoes Trials," *Jane's Defense Weekly*, April 11, 2005.

14. Gareth Jennings, "Algeria Selects Merlin, Super Lynx Helos," *Jane's Defense Weekly*, November 21, 2007.

15. Vladimir Petrov, "Algeria Suspends Russian Arms Package," *Jane's Defense Weekly*, February 15, 2008.

16. This discussion draws heavily on interviews and the details provided in *Jane's Fighting Ships, 2007–2008*, plus other data from Jane's Information Group, London, and the country section in IISS, *Military Balance*, various editions.

17. J.A.C. Lewis, "Algeria Negotiates on FREMM Acquisition," *Jane's Defense Weekly*, February 22, 2008.

Figure 3.1 Algerian Force Trends, 1985–2008

Category/Weapon	1985	1990	1995	2000	2002	2004	2005	2006	2007	2008
DEFENSE BUDGET (US$2008 billions)	0.938	1.01	1.36	1.9	2.1	2.8	2.9	3.09	3.69	-
MOBILIZATION BASE										
Men Ages 13–17 (In thousands)	-	1,535	1,796	1,891	1,986	1,986	-	-	-	-
Men Ages 18–22 (In thousands)	-	1,328	1,551	1,693	1,934	1,834	-	-	-	-
MANPOWER										
Total Active	170,000	125,000	121,700	122,000	124,000	127,500	127,500	137,500	137,500	147,000
(Conscripts)	100,000	70,000	90,000	75,000	75,000	75,000	75,000	75,000	75,000	80,000
Total Reserve	150,000	150,000	150,000	150,000	150,000	150,000	150,000	150,000	150,000	150,000
Total	320,000	275,000	271,700	272,000	274,000	277,500	277,500	287,500	287,500	297,000
Paramilitary	30,550	23,000	105,000	146,200	181,200	181,200	181,200	181,200	187,200	187,200
LAND FORCES										
Active Manpower	150,000	107,000	105,000	105,000	107,000	110,000	110,000	120,000	120,000	127,000
(Conscripts)	100,000	70,000	90,000	75,000	75,000	75,000	75,000	75,000	75,000	80,000
Reserve Manpower	-	150,000	150,000	-	150,000	150,000	150,000	150,000	150,000	150,000
Total Manpower	-	257,000	255,000	-	257,000	260,000	260,000	270,000	270,000	277,000
Main Battle Tanks	700	900	960	951	1,089	1,000	1,000	920	920	895
AIFVs/Armored Cars/Lt. Tanks	800	1,055	1,035	1,000	1,174	989	989	1,084	1,084	1,040
APCs/Recces/Scouts	550	860	460	680+	945	903	903	1,049	1,049	840
ATGM Launchers	-	-	-	-	-	-	-	-	-	200+

(continued)

Figure 3.1 *(continued)*

Category/Weapon	1985	1990	1995	2000	2002	2004	2005	2006	2007	2008
SP Artillery	100	120	185	185	185	185	185	170	170	170
Towed Artillery	550	390	405	416	418	406	406	375	375	375
MRLs	170	78	126	126	96	144	144	144	144	144
Mortars	180	-	330	330	330+	330+	330+	330	330	330
SSM Launchers	-	-	-	-	-	-	-	-	-	-
AA Guns	280+	855	895	895	980	899	899	875	875	875
Lt. SAM Launchers	-	-	-	1,000+	1,000+	1,000+	1,000+	288+	288+	288+
AIR & AIR DEFENSE FORCES										
Active Manpower	12,000	12,000	10,000	10,000	10,000	10,000	10,000	10,000	10,000	14,000
Reserve Manpower	-	-	-	-	-	-	-	-	-	-
Aircraft										
Total Fighters/FGA/Recces	332	257	170	181	166	175	175	212	212	141
Bombers	0	0	0	0	0	0	0	0	0	0
Fighters	110	146	100	110	114	83	83	124	124	55
FGA	150	47	50	50	48	66	66	76	76	78
COIN/OCU	0	18	0	0	0	0	0	0	0	0
Recces	6	3	9	10	10	12	12	12	12	8
Airborne Early Warning (AEW)	0	0	0	0	0	0	0	0	0	0
Electronic Warfare (EW)	0	0	0	0	0	0	0	0	0	0
Maritime Patrol	8	2	2	15	15	15	15	15	15	6
Combat-Capable Trainers	39	60	11	8	10	10	10	43	43+	89
Tankers	0	0	0	0	0	0	0	6	6	6
Transport	29	26	26	27	27	27	27	38	38	38

(continued)

Figure 3.1 (continued)

Category/Weapon	1985	1990	1995	2000	2002	2004	2005	2006	2007	2008
Helicopters										
Attack/Armed/ASW	35	38	60	65	63	93	91	33	33	33
Other	72	91	53	63	50	50	50	142	142	142
Total	107	129	113	138	138	143	142	175	175	175
SAM Forces										
Batteries	5	9	9	9	9	9	9	-	-	-
Heavy Launchers	44	51	51	43	43	43	43	140+	140+	140+
NAVAL FORCES										
Active Manpower	8,000	6,500	6,700	7,000	7,000	7,500	7,500	7,500	7,500	6,000
Reserve Manpower	-	-	-	-	-	-	-	-	-	-
Total Manpower	8,000	6,500	6,700	7,000	7,000	7,500	7,500	7,500	7,500	6,000
Submarines	2	4	2	2	2	2	2	2	2	2
Destroyers/Frigates/Corvettes	7	6	6	6	8	9	9	9	9	9
Missile	4	3	3	3	5	6	6	9	9	9
Other	3	3	3	3	3	3	3	0	0	0
Missile Patrol	8	11	11	11	9(2)	9(2)	9(2)	9	9	9
Coastal/Inshore Patrol	-	11	8	5	3	10	10	13	13	11
Mine	1	1	1	1	0	0	0	0	0	0
Amphibious Ships	3	3	3	3	3	3	3	3	3	3
Landing Craft/Light Support	-	-	-	6	6	6	6	6	6	13
ASW/Combat Helicopters	-	-	-	0	0	0	0	0	0	0

Source: Adapted by Anthony H. Cordesman from data provided by U.S. experts, and from the International Institute for Strategic Studies, *The Military Balance*, various editions.

Note: Figures in parentheses are additional equipment in storage or not operational. SSM launchers are major systems. "0" connotes that a zero number has been verified, whereas "-" connotes that data are not known or verifiable.

4

THE MILITARY FORCES OF LIBYA

Libya has sought to shed its image as an extremist state and supporter of terrorism in recent years. It reached a settlement on its terrorist attacks on UTA and Pan Am passenger aircraft, and has halted all support of terrorist groups. In late 2003, it agreed to give up its efforts to acquire and deploy WMD and consented to inspection by the IAEA. Libya did so partly because of years of frustration and failure in various political and military adventures and partly because of the impact of UN and U.S. sanctions, growing economic problems, and the need to deal with a low-level Islamic extremist insurgent threat.

The Libyan armed forces have also been sharply affected by head of state Muammar Qadhafi's eccentricities and by his past efforts to eliminate military ranks and create a people's army. The forces are divided into an army, navy, and air force, but large numbers of men and women have at least a paper assignment to paramilitary forces such as the People's Militia, Revolutionary Guards Corps, and People's Cavalry Force. The army operates Libya's surface-to-surface missile forces, the national air defense command is part of the air force, and the navy controls the coast guard.

The trends in Libyan military forces are shown in **Figure 4.1**. On paper, Libya still retains large military assets. Libya's land forces have a total of 2,025 tanks, more than 1,000 AIFVs, 945 APCs, 444 SP artillery, more than 647 towed artillery, and 830 MRLs. Its air forces possess 374 combat-capable aircraft and 35 attack helicopters. Its naval forces have two submarines, three major surface ships, 14 patrol craft, four mine warfare ships, and four amphibious ships. These totals are impressive for a relatively small country, but much of this force is in storage or non-operational, combat readiness is exceptionally low, and modernization rates are very poor.

Libya still suffers from the impact of its military buildup during the 1970s and 1980s. Libya acquired a vast weapons inventory that it could not man or operate, turning the country into the world's largest military parking lot. This gross military overexpansion was then followed by international sanctions on Libya—including sanctions governing the sale of new military equipment, spare parts, and upgrades for older systems. As a result, the "parking lot" became filled with military obsolescence.

This situation is beginning to change as a result of normalization between Libya and the international community. France, Italy, Russia, and the United Kingdom have positioned themselves to cash in on Libya's renewed permit to buy arms. France hopes to sell an initial 14 Rafales to Libya. Russia is poised to offer Libya new air capabilities, and moved to cancel Libya's $4.5 billion Soviet-era debt in April 2008.[1] The United States lifted on the last remaining bans on commercial activity in 2004, but has yet to authorize U.S. companies to export arms and equipment to the former pariah state.

Until Libya's efforts to acquire more weapons systems materialize, Libya's military forces will remain a military farce. Libya's neighbors cannot, however, count on the permanence of the "parking lot syndrome," overlook the sheer mass of Libya's arms holdings, or ignore Libya's efforts to acquire new systems and upgrades for obsolescent ones. Libya has the ability to engage in costly and prolonged confrontations and clashes in the border area with its other neighbors.

At the same time, Libya, like Algeria and Morocco, faces an increasingly tangible threat from Islamist extremist groups. As a result, Libya's military and paramilitary forces focus on repressing both progressive and militant Islamist movements. The most important of these is the Libyan Islamic Fighting Group (LIFG), which became affiliated with al Qaeda in November 2007 and receives support from Algeria's AQIM, especially in the vicinity of Benghazi and Derna in the east of the country.[2]

LIBYAN ARMY

The Libyan Army has a total active strength of only 50,000 men, including something approaching 25,000 badly trained conscripts. Although the army is sometimes reported to have some 40,000 men in the People's Militia, this force is more a symbol of Qadhafi's ever-changing ideology than a military force. The Revolutionary Guards Corps is at most a brigade-sized force with about 3,000 men and equipped with tanks, APCs, ATGWs, air defense weapons, and helicopters. The People's Cavalry Force is a largely token force. The Libyan Army seems to lack anything approaching an effective and well-trained reserve system.

Reports differ sharply over the organization of Libyan ground forces. The International Institute for Strategic Studies (IISS), which seems to be the most credible source, reports that the Libyan Army is organized into 11 border defense zones and four security zones and has one elite regime security brigade, 10 tank battalions, 10 mechanized infantry battalions, 18 infantry battalions, six paratrooper/paracommando battalions, four surface-to-surface missile brigades, 22 artillery battalions, and seven air defense artillery battalions. Another source indicates that the army is organized into 2–3 tank divisions, 2–4 mechanized infantry divisions, two independent tank brigades, and two independent mechanized brigades. It also has three independent tank battalions, eight mechanized infantry battalions, a Republican Guard brigade, 12–13 paracommando battalions, seven surface-to-surface missile brigades, three SAM brigades, 41 artillery battalions, and two anti-aircraft (AA) gun battalions.

Regardless of the exact totals, Libya only has about 25–33 percent of the manpower needed to man its strength of combat units and total equipment pool—a factor that explains why so much of its major combat equipment is in storage. Even its best combat units are under strength and have severe training and leadership problems. These manpower problems are compounded by tight political control, promotion based on political favoritism, and training that is often limited to erratic small-unit training. Qadhafi also rotates officers arbitrarily to prevent coup attempts and restricts some forms of training because he regards them as a threat to his security. Libya's seeming return to the international community is unlikely to change this pattern. Additionally, the resumption of Libya sending 6–8 cadets annually to Poland's Warsaw-based military academy of technology is a token gesture at best, having a negligible impact on overall force quality, and is a far cry from the scale of structural and ideological change needed for army-wide impact.

As of 2008, the Libyan Army had some 2,025 MBTs. Its operational holdings, however, only included some 800 MBTs: 200 T-72s, 100 T-62s, and 500 T-55s. The other 1,225 tanks, including about 1,040 T-55s, 70 T-62s, and 115 T-72s, have been in storage for at least the past five years. Many of both the operational and stored tanks had significant maintenance problems, and Libya was actively negotiating with Russia and the Ukraine in 2000 for modernization and overhaul contracts for these tanks as well as for its other armor and much of its artillery. As of mid-2008, these efforts have yet to bear fruit, and it is not unreasonable to expect that Libya will continue to maintain obsolescent MBTs at least through 2009.

The army had some 120 aging armored reconnaissance vehicles, including 50 BDRM-2s and 70 EE-9 Cascavals, a small portion of the number Libya had originally purchased. It possessed more than 1,000 aging BMP-1 AIFVs and about 945 APCs, including 750 BTR-50s and BTR-60s, 67 OT-62s and OT-64s, 28 M-113s, and 100 EE-11 Urutus. These holdings represented far too many types of APCs to allow for effective support and maintenance. Their armament and armor were often dated, low quality, and worn. Like Libya's tanks, many of its other armored vehicles were in storage or had serious maintenance problems. Only a few battalion-sized elements of Libyan armor had even moderate effectiveness in offensive and maneuver operations.

Libya's artillery strength included some 647 major towed artillery weapons, 444 SP artillery weapons, and 830 MRLs—many of which are not operational. The towed weapons included 42 105-mm M-101s, 190 D-30 and 60 D-74 122-mm weapons, 330 130-mm M-46 weapons, and 25 M-1937 152-mm weapons. The SP artillery included 130 2S1 122-mm weapons, 160 Palmaria and 14 M-109 155-mm weapons, and 60 2S3 and 80 DANA 152-mm weapons. Libya's MRLs included 300 Type 63 107-mm and 200 BM-11, 230 BM-21, and 100 RM-70 122-mm weapons. Libya also had more than 500 82-mm and 120-mm mortars and some M-160 160-mm mortars. The army also had about 45 FROG-7 surface-to-surface missile launchers. (Some unconfirmed reports indicate an additional 80 Scud Bs and 450–500 North Korean No Dong missiles.)

This artillery strength was numerically impressive, but once again, much of it was in storage or non-operational. Libya had poor standardization in terms of weapon and ammunition types. It also lacked the training, organization, and sensors and C⁴ equipment to conduct combined arms operations, maneuver effectively, switch fires rapidly, target beyond visual range, and conduct efficient counterbattery operations. Libya signed a deal with the United Kingdom in May 2008 to acquire tactical communications and data systems and accompanying support training. The system is similar to the British military's Bowman kit and is meant for Libya's mechanized Elite Brigade. It is as yet unclear whether Libya will seek to equip other elements of the army with similar equipment, in which case it would still be unclear whether Libya could make good use of them to augment its C⁴ capabilities.[3]

Libya's anti-tank weapons included roughly 3,000 ATGW launchers, with 400 Milans, 40 9P122 BRDM-2 Saggers, 620 AT-3 Saggers, and an additional 1,940 AT-3s mounted on BDRMs, AT-4 Spigots, and AT-5 Spandrels. These ATGWs are effective against any tank other than the M-1A and possibly the T-80, but Libya does not normally provide effective live-fire training under realistic conditions. France and Libya signed a deal in July 2007 to provide the army with Milan ADT-ER ATGMs and Tetra communications equipment, but it is unclear whether these systems have been delivered.[4] The army also had at least 220 M-40A1 106-mm recoilless rifles and large numbers of anti-tank rocket launchers.

Nothing approaching an accurate count of Libya's operational light air defense weapons is available. Some estimates indicate that the army had an inventory of about 490 air defense guns as of 2008, including 250 radar-guided ZSU-23-4 23-mm SP guns, and its towed systems included 100 ZPU-2 14.5-mm weapons, some M-53 and M-59 30-mm weapons, 50 L/70 40-mm weapons, and 90 S-60 57-mm weapons. Libya also had 400 SA-7, SA-9, and SA-13s, and 24 Quad Crotale light SAMs. Many of these weapons are stored or have limited operational readiness. The overall air defense training of Libyan army forces is poor. The army has O1-E liaison aircraft, which the air force could support with 55 transport and liaison helicopters. These include four CH-47s and 35 Mi8/Mi-17 transport helicopters, five AB-206s, and 11 SA-316s.

Libya's combat support, service support, and logistics units and system are capable of little more than sustaining peacetime garrison operations and occasional set-piece exercises. They would break down quickly in the event of war. The army seems to have no real training using support and logistics capabilities at even the major combat unit level.

In summary, Libya's army and paramilitary forces have little military effectiveness, and efforts to recapitalize its forces in recent years have yet to yield concrete results. Although a few regular army brigades and some independent elements may have moderate effectiveness, Libya can do comparatively little to make use of its massive inventory of land weapons. Training and readiness are very poor. Libya's erratic equipment purchases make logistics, support, and maintenance a military nightmare. Some purchases seem to be made with no regard to whether the equipment will have any military utility or can be absorbed into Libya's force structure. Nearly one-half of the army's equipment is in storage or has limited operational availability, and overall leadership and organization are poor. Even Libya's better units would have difficulty fighting anything other than static defensive battles.

LIBYAN NAVY

The Libyan Navy and Coast Guard have a nominal strength of 8,000 men but may only have 4,000–4,100 actives. The navy has significant combat ship strength but little real-world war-fighting capability for anything more than surprise or hit-and-run missions. Maintenance and manpower readiness are poor. It has little ability to operate outside of coastal waters, and its sea training and patrol activity are far below the level needed for high military proficiency. It cannot count on significant air support in an encounter with a Western navy, and has negligible offensive capability beyond launching a few missiles.[5]

Jane's Defense Weekly reports that the navy has its headquarters at Surt; naval bases at Al Khums and Tobruq; a submarine base at Ras Hilal; a naval air station at Al Girdabiyah; a naval infantry battalion at Sidi Bilal; and working ports at Benghazi, Derna, and Tripoli. IISS reports that Libya has major facilities at Benghazi, Khums Tbruk, and Tripoli in addition to minor bases at Derna, Misonhah, and Zuwurah.[6]

The Libyan Navy's main combat forces consist of two aging Foxtrot-class fleet submarines (six were delivered, but all seem to be non-operational), two guided missile frigates, one missile corvette, 14 missile patrol craft (a number in semi–non-operational reserve), four coastal patrol craft for constabulary duties, and four ocean minesweepers. Libya also had five landing ships (two in reserve), three landing craft tanks (LCTs), one training ship, one support ship, one diving ship, 10 transport ships, one salvage ship, two floating docks, and seven coastal tugs.

Libya has done a poor job of creating operational naval forces. Libya at one point had six 1,950-ton ex-Soviet Foxtrot-class submarines that were delivered between 1976 and 1982. These were export versions of the submarine from a reactivated production line and were obsolescent when delivered. They were armed with 533-mm torpedo tubes and had Soviet Type 53 active/passive and SEAT-60 passive homing torpedoes (15-km range) homing torpedoes. They were only fully operational as long as the Soviet Union trained and supported the crews and maintained the ships before the end of the Cold War. This does not seem to have been the case since 1984, and there have been no regular undersea patrols since that time. One submarine sank in 1993. It was raised but not returned to service. Libya was seeking to overhaul and modernize its remaining submarines when the UN sanctions were imposed, but its remaining ships are now so obsolete that there is little point in such modernization. Only two of its submarines are now operational, and only one, the *Al Khybedr*, makes occasional surface patrols. According to *Jane's Defense Weekly*, Russia might supply Libya with two Kilo-class diesel-electric submarines to compensate for Libya's obsolescent Foxtrots, but as of mid-2008 Russia and Libya had yet to solidify an arms deal, which could approach $2.2 billion.[7]

Libya retains two missile frigates: 1,900-ton ex-Soviet Koni-class vessels delivered in 1986 and 1987. Each was armed with four SS-N-2C Styx missiles (83-km range), four 76-mm guns, four twin 30-mm guns, SA-N-4 Gecko SAM launchers, and four 406-mm torpedo tubes. They could fire Soviet Type 40 active/passive antisubmarine torpedoes. These two frigates lack some of the sensors and electronics of Soviet ships but are relatively modern. Both ships are active, but have not had any significant modernization since they were delivered in the late 1980s. Libya's capability to fully operate these two ships in combat is uncertain.

Libya has 1–2 660-ton Soviet Nanuchka II–class corvette with four SS-N-2C missiles (83-km range), SA-N-4 Gecko SAM launchers, and two twin 57-mm guns. It originally had four. The U.S. Navy sank one on March 24, 1986. Another, the *Tariq Ibn Ziyad* (formerly the *Ean Mara*), was severely damaged by the U.S. Navy on March 25, 1986, but was repaired in the Soviet Union and returned to service. It and the *Ean Zara* seem to be quasi-operational. Another, the *Ean Al Gzala*, has not been at sea for four years and may have been stripped for parts.

Libya has 12 311-ton Combattante IIG–class missile patrol boats (six of which seem to be operational), delivered in 1982–1983. Each has four single Otomat Mark I/II launchers (60–80 km range) and one 76-mm gun. Only some of these ships are crewed and operational. France and Libya began discussions in 2006 to upgrade as many as nine of the navy's Combattante IIGs. Libya's missile patrol craft also include four 245-ton OSA II–class boats, delivered in 1976–1980, each with four SS-N-2C Styx anti-ship missile launchers (83-km range) and two twin 30-mm guns. It is uncertain whether their anti-ship missiles are fully operational. Libya also received four Croatian-built PV30-LS fast patrol boats for its coast guard. The navy will receive 10 ships, which will play an increasing role in Libya's effort to improve maritime patrol and border surveillance to intercept smugglers and people traffickers. IISS reported that four of the ships were already in service in 2008.[8]

The navy still has at least four 804-ton Soviet Natya-class ocean-going minesweepers in inventory. These represent a moderate threat because they can lay mines with little warning. Yet, Libya has already used commercial cargo ships to lay mines in the Red Sea, and this kind of asymmetric warfare does not require combat ships. They are used for coastal patrols and training and have never been observed in minesweeping exercises.

The Libyan Navy has some four amphibious ships, including three LCTs in inventory. These ships include two 2,800-ton PS-700-class LSTs with a capacity of 240 troops and 11 tanks each. Both have not been modernized since the late 1970s but are operational. One, however, may have been transferred to commercial service. There are three Turkish-made 600-ton LCTs (with a capacity of 100 troops and five tanks each), but their operability is doubtful. Libya has a number of training and support ships. They include one 500-ton training ship, one support ship, a salvage ship, a diving tender, seven tugs, and 10 2,412-ton transport ships. These latter transport ships are now in commercial service, and can be used either to move heavy equipment and troops or to lay mines.

The navy has the support of two air force squadrons with a total of 32 armed helicopters, including 25 Mi-14 Haze ASW helicopters and seven SA-321 Frelon and SA-341 Super Frelon ASW and SAR helicopters. They are worn and obsolete, and most are not operational. They can carry AM-39 Exocets but do not seem to do so. The operational status of the Hazes is unclear. Five SA-316B support helicopters were assigned to support the police and customs service, but none now seem to be operational.

The air force assists the navy with naval reconnaissance and surface support. Libya is slated to receive one ATR-42MP maritime patrol craft to be provided by Italian firm Alenia Aeronautica. Equipped with a search radar, an electro-optical sensor, and airdrop equipment, this aircraft could augment the navy's coast patrol and SAR capabilities and should be delivered by 2009.[9]

In addition, the navy had at least one shore battery with SS-C-3 Styx missiles, and possibly additional batteries with Otomat and SS-N-2D missiles (95-km range). Libya also has some kind of coastal radar and surveillance system, and may be using part of its popular militia in a coast-watch mission.[10]

The Libyan Navy's overall training and readiness levels were never high, and declined sharply after the mid-1980s, possibly because of decreased funding and a resulting drop in support from the Soviet Union. The navy suffered badly from UN sanctions, but acquired some Ukrainian technical support in 1995 and received more parts deliveries and repairs after 1998. It has continued to emphasize upgrading its inshore and coastal capabilities rather than pursuing acquisitions of additional major surface combatants. Some individual ship crews have moderate capabilities, but overall training, readiness, and command standards are low, and weapons systems and combat electronics are rarely exercised. Libya cannot operate as an effective fleet. Maintenance seems to be as badly organized as most aspects of Libyan military activity.

As is the case of Algeria and Morocco, the Libyan Navy has increasingly moved to take part in naval exercises in the Mediterranean, most recently with the U.S. 6th Fleet and other NATO and non-NATO countries. Algeria recently took part in Phoenix Express 2008. Bringing together naval assets from Algeria, France, Greece, Italy, Malta, Mauritania, Morocco, Portugal, Spain, Turkey, Tunisia, and the United States, the exercise emphasized joint training in surveillance, patrolling, SAR, and counterinsurgency operations.[11] Operations bringing together Algeria, Libya, Morocco, and Tunisia are constructive developments given past antagonisms and Libya's former pariah status in particular.

LIBYAN AIR FORCE

As of mid-2008, Libya's air force and air defense command had a nominal strength of 18,000 men. The air force had approximately 374 combat-capable aircraft and 35 armed helicopters. It had at least 10 large air bases with shelters and land-based antiaircraft defenses. It had major air bases at Banghazi-Banina, Benghazi, El Adem (General Abdel Nasser), Tripoli (Okba Ibn Nafa), Umm Aitqah, and Zawiyat-El Bayda. Libya's forces are concentrated at bases in Benghazi and Tripoli. There are dispersal bases at Ghat, Sebha, and Tobruk.

Libya's air force includes some advanced aircraft types, but much of it is obsolete or ineffective. The Libyan Air Force still has one bomber regiment with six Tu-22 Blinders. The USSR transferred 12 long-range Tu-22 bombers in April 1979, and 5–6 may still be marginally operational.[12] These aircraft are obsolete medium altitude bombers that are very vulnerable both to air-to-air missiles and to SAM defenses.

Libya's air force has seven fighter ground-attack squadrons, an estimated nine fighter squadrons, two reconnaissance squadrons, an attack helicopter squadron, and numerous fixed- and rotary-wing helicopter units. Its squadrons are organized into regiments, some of which have both defense and attack missions but which are normally either strike/attack or air defense regiments.

The only Libyan Air Force unit with advanced combat aircraft was a single Su-24 strike/attack squadron with just six aircraft. Soviet transfers of 6–10 Su-24Ds in 1989 gave Libya a more serious long-range strike fighter, then one of the most advanced aircraft in the Soviet inventory. The Su-24 is a twin seat swing-wing aircraft that is roughly equivalent in terms of weight to the F-111, although it has nearly twice the thrust loading and about one-third more wing loading. It is deployed in five variants. Although it is not clear which variant Libya has received, it seems likely that it is the export version of the Su-24D.

It is unclear how much of the avionics and sensor equipment on the Russian version of the aircraft were actually included in the export version. Russia has also upgraded its Su-24s to the far more advanced SU-24Ms, which can carry Russia's more modern missiles and which has much more advanced targeting capability, and intended to replace the plane with the more modern Su-35. Even if the Libyan versions of the Su-24D do have all of the capabilities of the Russian version, their avionics will be based on designs that are nearly three decades old.

If Libya does have the Russian version of the Su-24D, the plane has a moderately sophisticated radar warning receiver, EW suite, and terrain avoidance radar. It also has satellite communications and an aerial refueling probe, and can deliver electro-optical, laser, and radar-guided bombs and missiles. The Su-24 can carry payloads of nearly

25,000 pounds and can operate missions with a 1,300-km radius when carrying 6,600 pounds of fuel. With a more typical 8,818-lb (4,000-kg) combat load, it has a mission radius of about 790 km in the LO-LO-LO profile, and 1,600 km in the LO-HI-LO profile.

Although such missions have little to do with Libya's current military priorities, the export version of the Su-24D can reach Chad, Egypt, and Italy with extended-range fuel tanks and airborne refueling. It could even reach Israel, although the latter mission would be demanding, would have to be flown out of an eastern base such as Benghazi, and would allow only a limited time over the target.[13]

The Su-24 can carry up to three AS-7 Kerry radio-command guided missiles (5-km range) or one AS-9. It can also carry a mix of Kyle anti-radiation missiles with passive radar guidance and an active radar fuse (90-km range), three AS-10 Karen passive laser-guided missiles with an active laser fuse (10-km range), and three AS-11 Kilter anti-radiation missiles with passive radar guidance and an active radar fuse (50-km range). Alternatively, it can carry up to three AS-12 Kegler anti-radiation missiles with passive radar guidance and an active radar fuse (35-km range), three AS-13 Kingposts, and three AS-14 Kedge semi-active laser-guided missiles with an active laser fuse (12-km range). The Su-24 also can carry demolition bombs, retarded bombs, cluster bombs, fuel air bombs, and chemical bombs.

Libya has acquired a limited long-range refueling capability in order to ease many of the problems that it would face in conducting such strikes. Although Libya did not get the modified IL-76 that it had originally sought from the USSR for refueling its Su-24s, it did get the technology that it needed to convert one of its C-130s into a tanker for airborne refueling from West German firms. Libya has experimentally refueled its Mirage F-1s and was seeking a modifiable cargo jet so that it would be able to refuel at higher speeds and without the maneuver problems inherent in trying to refuel a jet fighter from a propeller aircraft.

Libya's six additional fighter ground-attack units had a total of 40 MiG-23BNs, 15 MiG-23Us, 14 Mirage F-1ADs, and 53 Su-20/22s. Some sources indicate there also was still a counterinsurgency squadron with 30 J-1 Jastrebs in 2004–2005, but this cannot be verified. Libyan attack aircraft performed poorly in close air support and interdiction missions in Chad. No reports indicate that Libya has since developed effective training systems and facilities or has practiced meaningful exercises in low-altitude combat, air defense evasion, countermeasure penetration, or combined arms with the army. Libya did, however, have relatively modern AS-7, AS-9, and AS-11 Soviet air-to-surface missiles and some anti-radiation missiles. It had large stocks of unguided bombs, including napalm, and seems to have had some laser-guided bombs.

The Libyan Air Force had nine fighter squadrons equipped with a total of 15 Mirage F-1ED/BDs, 45 MiG-21s, 75 MiG-23 Flogger Es, 94 MiG-25s, and three MiG-25Us. These air defense fighters had aging avionics with limited capability but advanced air-to-air missiles such as the AA-2 Atoll, AA-6 Acrid, AA-7 Apex, AA-8 Aphid, R-530, and R-550 Magic. Only the Mirage F-1s and some MiG-25s had more than very limited long-range intercept and look-down shoot-down capabilities. Libya had major pilot training problems and had lost a number of aircraft to accidents.

Libyan air-to-air training levels and air combat tactics have remained far inferior to those of U.S. pilots and well-trained Middle Eastern pilots such as those of Egypt and Saudi Arabia. Libya has some 250 trainers including 115 L-39ZO Albatros, 15 MiG-23Us, three MiG-25Us, four Mirage 5DP30s, three Mirage F-1BDs, and some 150 SF-260WLs. Libya originally had 250 SF-260WLs, and Italian firm Alenia Aermacchi will overhaul 12 of the trainers by the end of 2008.[14] Despite a drive to improve training and training equipment, Libya seems to have a serious shortage of even mediocre combat pilots, and may be dependent on Russian and other foreign officers and technicians for effective ground-controlled intercepts. It still does not seem to be able to conduct effective electronic warfare.

Libya has two reconnaissance squadrons with four Mirage-5DRs and seven MiG-25Rs. If the MiG-25R is similar to former Soviet versions, it has infrared, side-looking radar, and ESM capabilities. Libya also has some remotely piloted vehicles. This gives Libya a reasonable mix of basic reconnaissance capabilities, but it seems doubtful that it has organized to use them effectively. It may well rely on the slow daylight photography system of most developing nations.[15]

Libya had an attack helicopter squadron with 23 Mi-25s and 12 Mi-35s. Some of these helicopter forces seemed to have moderate training, but the helicopters were equipped with obsolescent avionics and with AT-2 Swatter air-to-ground missiles. Readiness was poor and some aircraft were lost to accidents. By mid-2008, a deal between France and Libya had almost been reached on the sale of an as of then unspecified number of the Eurocopter AS-665 Tiger multi-role combat helicopter. Russia has also offered to sell Libya modern combat helicopters, including the Kamov Ka-50 and Ka-52. Whichever system Libya ultimately selects, it will represent a major increase in helicopter attack capability.[16] Yet, it remains to be seen whether Libya can muster adequate personnel, training, and support to utilize such systems.

Other air units included seven transport squadrons, transport helicopters, and training aircraft. The transport squadrons had 23 An-26s, 15 CH-130s, two L-100-20s, three L-100-30s, six G-222s, 25 IL-76s, and 15 L-410s. There was a heavy transport helicopter squadron with four CH-47Cs, 46 Mi-2s, a medium transport squadron with 35 Mi-8s and Mis-17s, and a light unit with 11 SA-316s and five AB-206s. The transport forces seemed to be the most effective element of the air force.

These holdings are impressive in terms of sheer numbers, but the air force still has severe shortages of competent pilots, and training levels and quality are poor. The overall readiness of Libyan aircraft is poor, and most aircraft are now dated or obsolescent in terms of avionics and upgrades. The operational sustainability of even Libya's most combat-ready aircraft is limited, and most bases can evidently only support limited numbers of different aircraft types.

Libya reached a deal with France in 2006 to bring 12 of Libya's original 25 Mirage F-1s to operational status. The refurbishing deal would restore flight electronics and airframes as well as add new engines. The update package is not dissimilar from the ASTRAC upgrade suite, which is currently under way to update Moroccan Mirage F-1s. Updating Libya's F-1s will not be complete before 2009, and France seems to be opting to minimize the offer of a major upgrade suit in the hopes that Libya will buy 14 Dassault Rafales. Russia also hopes to make a major sale to Libya, offering 12 Su-35 Flanker multi-role fighters and potentially Su-30MK2s and MIG-29SMTs. French sources reported in June 2008 that Libya was more inclined to acquire the Rafale, but this remains to be confirmed, and as with its attack helicopters, it is not clear if Libya has the personnel and support infrastructure to make proper use of such modern systems.[17]

The air force seems to be dependent on foreign technicians for training, maintenance, and sometimes even combat missions. Overhaul and combat repair capability is limited, and combat sustainability is poor. Maintenance is mediocre, and an overcentralized and politicized command structure limits air defense proficiency and makes it difficult to effectively plan coherent air attacks and sustain significant numbers of sorties.

Despite growing efforts to recapitalize its air force, up to one-half of Libya's aircraft were in storage or of negligible operational value as of 2008, and the air force still seemed to rely heavily on North Korean, Pakistani, Syrian, and former Soviet "instructors" to fly actual missions.

LIBYAN LAND-BASED AIR DEFENSES

Libya's land-based air defenses are badly dated and are largely obsolete or obsolescent. They are, however, among the largest such defenses in the Middle East. In 2008, Libya's air defense forces included four SA-5 brigades, each with two battalions of six launchers (48 total), four air defense gun batteries, and a radar company. According to some reports, Russian personnel manned these SA-5 units in the past.

As of 2008, Libya had five regional SAM commands, each with five to six brigades with 18 SA-2 launchers each (160–180 launchers total), 2–3 brigades with 12 SA-3 launchers each (100–110 launchers total), 4 brigades with SA-5 launchers, and three brigades with 20-24 SA-6s (130–150 launchers) and some SA-8s. These missile units were loosely integrated by Libya's Senezh air defense and command system. Both the SAM units and command system of the air defense command were heavily dependent on expatriate support personnel, who sometimes seemed to act as operators. Overall capability was low, except for those forces with direct foreign "supervision."

Libya's major SAM forces were first placed under an air defense command, which was formed in 1973, the year of the October War. This command was merged and reorganized in the late 1980s after the U.S. air strikes on Libya. The air defense command seemed to be somewhat more effective than the air force. As of 2000, it was reasonably well deployed and provided overlapping coverage by a range of different missiles along the coastal areas. The network of radars was badly dated, however, as were its EW and command and control assets.

If British reports are correct, Libya still uses a modification of the same kind of central command center and regional sector operations centers that the Soviet Union set up in Algeria, Iraq, Syria, and many other countries dependent on Soviet arms and aid. The Libyan system, however, was upgraded more than Algeria's was before the breakup of the Soviet Union. A high-capacity Soviet communications system was installed, and buried landlines are used extensively to reduce the system's electronic and physical vulnerability. The air defense command also seems to have been upgraded with relatively modern early-warning radars and EW equipment.

These problems led Libya to make the acquisition of new SAMs a key priority once UN sanctions were suspended in April 1999. Libya sought a new air defense system from Russia based on the S-300PMU1 and S-300PMU2 air defense missiles and their supporting radars and C^4 systems. Price was still a major issue during the Russian-Libyan negotiations in 2000, however, and Libya evidently looked at Belarus and Ukrainian versions of the same system.[18]

Russia renewed its efforts to provide Libya with new air defense systems in 2006–2008, offering the Tor-M2E (SA-15 Gauntlet) short-range air defense system in addition to the S-300PMU2 major SAM, the S125 Pechora (SA-3 Goa), and the Osa-AKM (SA-8 Gecko). A deal had not been reached as of mid-2008; however, Russia cancelled Libya's $4.5 billion debt in exchange for military, energy, and construction contracts.[19]

While acquiring new major SAM and other air defense systems is a major priority, the obsolescence of Libya's aging Soviet-supplied SAMs is scarcely its only problem. Operator training and proficiency remains low. The system is overcentralized and has relatively slow data processing and limited automated analysis capability. Ergonomics and data interfaces are poor, and the system is vulnerable to EW and anti-radiation missiles. Overall alert rates are poor to mediocre, and Libyan operators have not fully adapted to the use of Soviet automated systems. It is also unlikely that Libya's EW assets give it much protection against the level of jamming and countermeasure technology that the United States deployed in Operation Desert Storm, Operation Desert Fox, and Operation Iraqi Freedom.

LIBYAN PARAMILITARY AND SECURITY FORCES

Like most North African states, Libya is better at internal repression than at dealing with foreign threats. Libya has a number of paramilitary forces and security services. They act as a means of controlling the power of the regular military and providing Qadhafi with security.

The data on such forces is uncertain, and sources report very different details. There seems to be a 3,000-man Revolutionary Guard

Corps (Liwa Haris Al-Jamahirya) to guard Qadhafi with T-54/55/62 tanks, armored cars, APCs, MRLs, and ZSU-23-4s and SA-8s, which are taken from the army inventory. There also seem to be up to 2,500 men in the Islamic Pan African Legion, which may have one armored, one infantry, and one paracommando brigade, although its total manpower strength could only man less than one brigade slice. The Islamic Pan African Legion has at least 75 T-54s and T-55s and some EE-9 mechanized infantry combat vehicles. Roughly 700–1,000 men from the Islamic Pan African Legion were believed to be in the Sudan in 1988, but current deployments are unknown. There is also a people's cavalry force that acts largely as a parade unit, and a people's militia with a nominal strength of about 40,000 men.

As is the case with other North African states, there are comparatively little reliable data on the operations of the government's security forces. The best unclassified reporting comes from the State Department, and much of that reporting provides reliable insights into the operations of the security forces. The State Department reports that Libya maintains an extensive security apparatus consisting of several elite military units, including Qadhafi's personal bodyguards, local revolutionary committees, and people's committees, as well as the "purification" committees, which were formed in 1996. The result is a multilayered, pervasive surveillance system that monitors and controls the activities of individuals. In a twist of irony, Libya's internal paranoia might be the most effective means of dealing with what is increasingly looking like a common threat to Algeria, Morocco, Tunisia, and Libya from transnational jihadist groups operating both regionally and internationally.

NOTES

1. Stefan Marx, "Russia's Debt Deal with Libya Clears Way for Weapon Sales," *Jane's Missiles and Rockets*, May 2, 2008.

2. "Stirring of Islamic Radicalism in Libya," *Jane's Islamic Affairs Analyst*, July 26, 2005; "Intelligence Pointers – Libyan Group Gives Allegiance to Al-Qaeda," *Jane's Intelligence Digest*, November 13, 2007.

3. Andrew Chuter, "Libya Purchases Gear from General Dynamics UK," *Defense News*, May 8, 2008.

4. J.A.C. Lewis, "France Agrees Libyan Arms Sale," *Jane's Defense Industry*, August 3, 2007.

5. This discussion draws heavily on interviews and the details provided in *Jane's Fighting Ships, 2007–2008*; Jane's Information Group, London, and the

country section in the International Institute for Strategic Studies (IISS), *The Military Balance, 2008.*

6. See the country section for Libya in International Institute for Strategic Studies (IISS), *The Military Balance, 2008.*

7. J.A.C. Lewis, "Libya Nears Arms Deal with Russia," *Jane's Defense Weekly*, May 16, 2007.

8. Alex Paper, "Libya Acquires PV-30-LS Craft for Littoral Policing Role," *Jane's Navy International*, October 24, 2007; and the country section in IISS, *The Military Balance, 2008.* pp. 253–254.

9. Gareth Jennings, "Libya Places Maritime Patrol Aircraft Order with Alenia Aeronautica," *Jane's Defense Industry*, January 17, 2008.

10. This is a report from one source and the country section in IISS, *The Military Balance*, 2008. The creation of a coast watch seems erratic even for Libya.

11. Associated Press "Greece: Libya, France to Join U.S. Naval Exercises," *Defense News*, April 1, 2008.

12. Reports that Libya acquired 12 Soviet SS-12M (SS-22) missiles between mid-1980 and mid-1981 do not seem accurate. See Yossef Bodansky and Vaughn Forrest, *Chemical Weapons in the Third World*, U.S. House Task Force on Terrorism and Unconventional Warfare, May 29, 1990, p. 4; House Republican Research Committee, "Libya's Chemical-Biological Warfare Capabilities," June 12, 1990, p. 3; Martin Sicker, *The Making of a Pariah State* (New York: Praeger, 1987), pp. 104–105; John K. Colley, *Libyan Sandstorm* (New York: Holt, Rinehart, and Winston, 1982), pp. 248–251.

13. *Aviation Week and Space Technology*, April 10, 1989, pp. 19–20; *New York Times*, April 5, 1989, *New York Times*, September 7, 1989; *Washington Times*, January 16, 1989; FBIS/NES, April 10, 1989.

14. Michael J Gething, "Aermacchi Wins Overhaul Work on Libyan Trainers," *Jane's Defense Weekly*, August 6, 2007.

15. Foreign technicians could provide effective support in the use of radar reconnaissance data. The basic problems with daylight reconnaissance photography are that it is not as discriminating as radar or electro-optics, cannot be processed until the aircraft lands, takes several hours to process, and requires expert interpretation. This is adequate against static targets, but even infantry units often move too quickly to use such data for targeting purposes.

16. J.A.C. Lewis, "France to Refurbish Libyan Mirages," *Jane's Defense Weekly*, November 23, 2006; J.A.C. Lewis, "Libya nears arms deal with Russia," *Jane's Defense Weekly*, May 16, 2007.

17. Agence France Press, "France in Talks on Sale of 100 Rafale Jets," *Defense News*, June 16, 2008; J.A.C. Lewis, "Libya Nears Arms Deal with Russia," *Jane's Defense Weekly*, May 16, 2007.

18. "Libya's Armed Forces," *IISS Strategic Comments* 6, no. 10 (December 2000).

19. Stefan Marx, "Russia's Debt Deal with Libya Clears Way for Weapon Sales," *Jane's Missiles and Rockets*, May 2, 2008.

Figure 4.1 Libyan Force Trends, 1985–2008

Category/Weapon	1985	1990	1995	2000	2002	2004	2005	2006	2007	2008
DEFENSE BUDGET (US$2008 billions)	0.709	1.39	0.967	1.3	1.21	1.31	0.72	0.59	0.65	-
MOBILIZATION BASE										
Men Ages 13–17 (In thousands)	-	-	262,000	312,400	350,000	387,000	387,000	-	-	-
Men Ages 18–22 (In thousands)	-	-	216,000	262,200	291,000	320,000	320,000	-	-	-
MANPOWER										
Total Active	73,000	85,000	80,000	65,000	76,000	76,000	76,000	76,000	76,000	76,000
(Conscripts)	-	-	-	-	40,000	38,000	38,000	38,000	38,000	25,000
Total Reserve	-	40,000	40,000	40,000	40,000	40,000	40,000	40,000	40,000	40,000
Total Active + Reserve	-	125,000	120,000	105,000	116,000	116,000	116,000	116,000	116,000	116,000
Paramilitary	7,000	5,500	-	-	-	-	-	-	-	-
LAND FORCES										
Active Manpower	58,000	55,000	50,000	35,000	45,000	45,000	45,000	45,000	45,000	50,000
(Conscripts)	-	-	25,000	25,000	25,000	25,000	25,000	25,000	25,000	25,000
Reserve Manpower	-	-	-	-	-	-	-	-	-	-
Total Manpower	58,000	55,000	50,000	35,000	45,000	45,000	45,000	45,000	45,000	50,000
Main Battle Tanks	2,800	2,300	2,210	2,025	985	800	800	800	800 (1,225)	800 (1,225)
AIFVS/Armored Cars/Lt. Tanks	1,200	1,635	1,640	1,630	1,438	1,000	1,000	1,000+	1,000+	1,000+
APCs/Recces/Scouts/Half-Tracks	1,160	950	900	990	1,381	1,065	1,065	1,065	1,065	1,065
ATGM Launchers	3,000	3,000	3,000	3,000	3,000	3,000	3,000	3,000	3,000	3,000

(continued)

Figure 4.1 *(continued)*

Category/Weapon	1985	1990	1995	2000	2002	2004	2005	2006	2007	2008
SP Artillery	218	370	450	450	265	444	444	444	444	444
Towed Artillery	930	720	720	720	647	647	647	647+	647+	647+
MRLs	600	650	700	700	564	830	830	830	830	830
Mortars	450	-	-	-	-	500	500	500	500	500
SSM Launchers	48	120	120	120	120	120	125	125	125	45
AA Guns	350+	600+	600	600	600	600	600	600	600	490
Lt. SAM Launchers	-	-	-	1,000+	1,000+	2,500+	2,500+	24+	24+	424+
AIR & AIR DEFENSE FORCES										
Active Manpower	8,500	22,000	22,000	22,000	23,000	23,000	23,000	23,000	23,000	18,000
Reserve Manpower	-	-	-	-	-	-	-	-	-	-
Aircraft										
Total Fighters/FGA/Recces	535	513	417	420	360	400	380	356	356	356
Bombers	7	4	6	6	6	6	6	7	7	7
Fighters	285	284	209	212	177	209	189	229	229	229
FGA	204	206	164	194	172	172	172	113	113	113
Recces	7	13	12	11	11	11	11	7	7	7
COIN/OCU	30	30	30	0	0	0	0	0	0	0
Airborne Early Warning (AEW)	0	0	0	0	0	0	0	0	0	0
Electronic Warfare (EW)	0	0	0	0	0	0	0	0	0	0
Maritime Reconnaissance	0	0	0	0	0	0	0	0	0	0
Combat-Capable Trainers	14	-	-	231	218	206	206	140	230	230
Tankers	0	0	0	0	0	0	0	0	0	0
Transport	62	82	78	75	81	83	83	83	83	85+

(continued)

Figure 4.1 *(continued)*

Category/Weapon	1985	1990	1995	2000	2002	2004	2005	2006	2007	2008
Helicopters										
Attack/Armed/ASW	42	35	52	52	41	41	60	60	60	35
Other	55	89	98	98	112	90	90	104	104	101
Total	97	124	150	150	153	131	131	164	164	136
SAM Forces										
Batteries	12	33	39	39	39	39	39	36	36	36
Heavy Launchers	76?	150?	236	236	236	236	236	216+	204+	216+
NAVAL FORCES										
Active Manpower	6,500	8,000	8,000	8,000	8,000	8,000	8,000	8,000	8,000	8,000
Reserve Manpower	-	-	-	-	-	-	-	-	-	-
Total Manpower	6,500	8,000	8,000	8,000	8,000	8,000	8,000	8,000	8,000	8,000
Submarines	6	6	4	2	2	1(4)	1(4)	(2)	(2)	(2)
Destroyers/Frigates/Corvettes	10	10	6	7	5	2	2	3(3)	1(2)	1(2)
Missile	10	10	6	7	3	2	2	3(3)	1(2)	1(2)
Other	0	0	0	0	2	0	0	0	0	0
Missile Patrol	25	24	24	21	13(8)	8(22)	8(22)	14	14	10
Coastal/Inshore Patrol	5	23	8	8	8	-	-	-	-	4
Mine	7	8	8	8	6	2	2	5	5	4
Amphibious Ships	3	5	5	5	4(1)	3(2)	3(2)	8(3)	5	4
Landing Craft/Light Support	-	4+	10	10	12	12	12	15	18	16
ASW/Combat Helicopters	-	31	30	32	7	7	7	7	7	7

Source: Adapted by Anthony H. Cordesman from data provided by U.S. experts, and from the International Institute for Strategic Studies, *The Military Balance*, various editions.

Note: Figures in parentheses are additional equipment in storage or not operational. SSM launchers are major systems. Main battle tank totals as of 2002 do not include units in storage. "0" connotes that a zero number has been verified, whereas "-" connotes that data are not known or verifiable

5

THE MILITARY FORCES OF TUNISIA

Tunisia has always been a defensive military power. Until recently, its major threat has been Libya, but at this point it faces no serious external threat. However, as in the cases of Algeria, Libya, and Morocco, Tunisia has experienced an increase in jihadist activity. Its armed forces are designed largely for border defense, internal security, and protection of key economic facilities. Tunisia lacks the active force and equipment strength necessary to deploy significant strength on either border in peacetime, and keeps most of its units near urban centers. It does, however, have special units in the Sahara brigade that cover the border and provide a light screen of security forces. Again, as in the cases of its North African neighbors, Tunisia is increasingly involved in mainly maritime NATO exercises, intelligence gathering, and counterinsurgency training and operations.

The armed forces have a conventional organization and command structure, with a minister of defense and an army chief of staff and an army, national guard, navy, and air force. The trends in Tunisian military forces are shown in **Figure 5.1.** Tunisia had total force of only some 35,800 men as of 2008, including 22,000 conscripts. Its land forces had a total of 84 MBTs, 268 APCs, 60 Recces, and 115 pieces of towed artillery. Its air force possessed 27 combat aircraft and 12 attack helicopters. Its naval forces had 12 missile patrol craft and 13 other patrol boats. These small equipment holdings make Tunisia an exception to the militarism of most North African states. These force levels are far closer in size to Tunisia's real strategic needs than the force levels of any of its neighbors, but vulnerability is the price of moderation.

TUNISIAN ARMY

The Tunisian Army has a total of 27,000 men, of which some 22,000 are conscripts with limited experience and training. Officer and career soldier training and proficiency are moderate to good by developing world standards. Conscripts are selected to ensure that they have a good basic education, but only serve for 12 months. Overall training standards are physically rigorous, but conscripts gain little proficiency in combined arms and maneuver warfare. The total strength of Tunisia's organized reserves is currently unknown. There is little indication that they are well trained or organized or would be combat effective without months of reorganization and training.

The army was reorganized in the early 1990s to create three mechanized brigades, and the chain of command now flows down from the army chief of staff to the first, second, and third mechanized brigades, the Sahara brigade, and a special-forces brigade. The major Tunisian army base is in Tunis.

Each of the three mechanized brigades has one armored regiment, two mechanized infantry regiments, one artillery regiment, and one air defense regiment. One report indicates that a typical mechanized brigade is supposed to have a tank battalion with 42 MBTs; a mechanized battalion with 45 APCs; a motorized rifle battalion with 34 light armored vehicles; an artillery battalion with 18 guns; an ATGW battery with 12 fire units; an antiaircraft battalion; an engineer battalion; a reconnaissance company; and logistic, transport, and supply elements. The army also has one engineer regiment. These formations are generally relatively small. A Tunisian brigade generally has only about 5,000 men, and a regiment consists of only 1,000–1,500 men.

The army has slowly acquired 84 MBTs (30 M-60A1s and 54 M-60A3s). It has 48 obsolescent Steyr SK-105 Kuerassier light tanks and 60 relatively low-grade armored reconnaissance vehicles, including 24 Saladins and 40 AML-90s. It has about 268 APCs, including 140 M-113 A-1/2s, 18 EE-11 Urutus, and 110 Fiat F-6614s.

Tunisia is learning how to use modern armor, but is only capable of largely static defense in the event of a major attack by Algeria or Libya. Its armor is poorly standardized, and many items are aging or obsolete. Overall, Tunisian armored forces have continuing maintenance and standardization problems. They are trained well enough for light defensive operations, but have limited maneuver and offensive capability.

The army has made improvements in its artillery strength in recent years, and most Tunisian artillery battalions now seem to have a full complement of weapons. Total strength has gone from 83 artillery pieces in 1988 to about 117 weapons in 1995 and to 115 weapons by 2008, but this strength is all in towed weapons that cannot maneuver with armor. Tunisia has 48 M-101A1/A2 105-mm towed weapons, 12 M-114A1 155-mm towed weapons, and 55 M-198 155-mm towed weapons. It also has 95 81-mm mortars and 66 107-mm and 120-mm mortars. It has been able to employ these weapons defensively in small batteries, but has limited maneuver, command and control, counterbattery, and beyond visual range targeting capability.

The anti-tank weapons strength of the Tunisian Army is limited, although it includes some modern types such as the Milan and TOW. As of 2008, Tunisia had a mix of 500 Milan and 90 TOW ATGM launchers, including 35 TOW ATGM launchers mounted on M-901 armored vehicles. It also had 300 M-20 and 300 LRAC 89-mm anti-tank rocket launchers. Few anti-tank crews have high readiness or realistic training against mobile armor.

The air defense weapons of the Tunisian Army include 60 aging RBS-70 and 26 M-48 Chaparral SAM fire units. Tunisia also has 100 M-55 20-mm guns, 15 M-1939 Type 55/-65 37-mm AA guns, and 12 SP M-42 40-mm guns. These weapons are capable of providing limited low-altitude point defense. Tunisia has no heavy SAM systems in the army or the air force.

Tunisia is only beginning to acquire the elements of modern armored warfare training, and it faces massive problems in rationalizing its diverse inventory, which now consists of far too many erratic small buys of incompatible or difficult-to-support equipment. The army badly needs to improve its manpower management, emphasis on professionalism, career incentives, and support and logistics capabilities. At present, most units cannot operate effectively for any length of time unless they are near their peacetime depots and casernes. Even then. however, the logistics and service support system is not particularly effective.

TUNISIAN NAVY

The 4,800-man Tunisian Navy is based at Bizerte, Keliba, La Goulette, and Sfax, and ship crews tend to be relatively professional. As of mid-2008, its holdings included 12 missile fast attack craft, three regular fast attack craft, 10 inshore patrol craft, and six training/support/survey ships. Two more regular fast attack craft were on order, and a number of its patrol craft were not truly operational or were laid up.

The navy had three Combattante III-class 425-ton missile guided fast attack craft, each with two quad MM-40 Exocet anti-ship missile launchers. The Exocet missiles have active radar homing and a maximum range of 70 km (40 miles). They also have one 76-mm gun and two twin 40-mm Breda guns. The ships incorporate an air-to-surface search radar, but there are no SAM launchers. These ships were all delivered in the mid-1980s and need modernization and refits. Tunisia also had three Bizerte-class 250-ton missile patrol craft with eight Aerospatiale SS 12Ms and four 37-mm guns. The SS 12M is a very short-range missile (5.5 km or 3 nautical miles) with a small warhead. These Bizerte-class ships are operational but are badly in need of refits.

Other combat ships included six Albatros (Type 143B) missile fast attack crafts with two OTO Melara 76-mm/62 guns and two 533-mm torpedo tubes. While the Albatros has launchers for MM-38 Exocets, the missiles were not included in the sale of the vessels from Germany. There are also an additional three 120-ton Haizhui-class ex-Chinese fast attack craft, each with four 25-mm guns. These ships were delivered in the mid-1990s, and all are operational.

The navy had three 250-ton Bizerte-class large patrol craft with 20-mm guns that date back to the late 1970s but that have had their guns updated and are operational. The navy had 10 coastal patrol craft. These included four Istiklal-class 80-ton coastal patrol craft with twin 20-mm guns and surface search radars and six 38-ton coastal patrol craft with 20-mm guns. The remaining vessels included six Kondor-class 377-ton patrol craft with twin 25-mm guns and five Bremse-class 42-ton patrol craft with twin 14.5-mm guns, operated by the coast guard, plus 11 32-ton coastal patrol craft operated by customs, four Gabes-class 18-ton patrol boats, and six training/survey ships.

Although Tunisia is capable of operating most of its individual ships, it does not seem to be organized for any kind of fleet or combined arms operations. The Tunisian Navy is adequate for patrol missions in local waters but is not capable of engaging the navies of any of Tunisia's neighbors. It is not strong enough to survive an attack by the Algerian or Libyan navies. Overall logistic and maintenance capabilities seem to be limited.

At the same time, Tunisia can probably count on Egyptian, European, and/or U.S. naval support in the event of any offensive attack by its neighbors, none of whom can risk confronting these naval powers. The risk of an open confrontation is further mitigated by increased participation on the parts of Algeria, Libya, Morocco, and Tunisia in U.S.-led NATO maritime operations in the Mediterranean.

TUNISIAN AIR FORCE

The 4,000-man Tunisian Air Force (TAF) has slowly developed relatively effective manpower policies and is gradually developing the capability to train and retain competent pilots and air crews. It is expanding steadily, and had 27 combat-capable aircraft and 12 attack helicopters as of early 2008. Its main bases are in Bizerte–La Karouba, Bizerte–Sidi Ahmed, and Sfax–El Maou. Its forces are organized largely along squadron lines with air defense, counterinsurgency, and attack training.

The TAF has done a good job of absorbing and operating its 12 F-5E/Fs in the fighter ground-attack role, and has gradually developed a limited capability for daytime air-to-air combat. It is unclear whether Tunisia still suffers from a shortage of trained F-5 pilots, but the F-5 is now an obsolescent aircraft at best, and is far inferior in combat capability in comparison with modern combat aircraft. Tunisia's F-5s can only be effective in attack missions against troops that are not equipped with modern man-portable or short-range guided missiles—a limitation that could present serious problems if the TAF must deal with regular Libyan forces. Tunisia badly needs 12–24 modern combat aircraft. Given potential threats, it needs a modern all-weather air defense fighter with beyond visual range air-to-air intercept capabilities.

The TAF also had three MB-326s in the counterinsurgency role. Some of its three MB-326B and 12 L-59 training aircraft seem to have limited combat capability. These planes, however, are at best capable of providing light ground support in a permissive environment where the enemy does not have effective AA guns or SAMs.

The air force has two S-208M liaison aircraft and a training wing with 14 combat capable SF-260s, four MB-326s, and 12 L-59s. It also has a wing with 42 helicopters, including six SA-313s, three SA-316s, 15 AB-205s, 12 UH-1s, and six AS-350Bs. These helicopters give Tunisia's armed forces considerable tactical air mobility for a force of their size.

In broad terms, Tunisia has a primitive air control and warning system and limited sensor coverage of Tunisian airspace. It is not organized to fight at the air force level, as distinguished from the formation or squadron level. It has the same problems in terms of retaining and training good personnel that the army does, and it is heavily reliant on foreign contractors for logistics and maintenance. Some effort has been made to give the TAF a combined operations capability based on U.S. doctrine and training concepts, but success is evidently still very limited.

TUNISIAN PARAMILITARY AND SECURITY FORCES

Tunisia's paramilitary forces consist of a national guard with 12,000 men. It has a naval element with some 30 patrol craft and an aerial element with eight SA-318 and SA-319 helicopters. The Tunisian National al Guard shares responsibility for internal security with the police. The police operate in the capital and a few other cities. In outlying areas, their duties are shared with or ceded to the national guard. Both forces are under the control of the minister of interior and the president.

As is the case with other North African states, there is comparatively little reliable detailed data on the operations of the government's security forces. The best unclassified reporting comes from the State Department, and much of this reporting provides reliable insight into the operations of the security forces.

Figure 5.1 Tunisian Force Trends, 1985–2008

Category/Weapon	1985	1990	1995	2000	2002	2004	2005	2006	2007	2008
DEFENSE BUDGET (2008 US$billions)	0.437	0.388	0.262	0.340	0.332	0.447	0.430	0.443	0.5	-
MOBILIZATION BASE										
Men Ages 13–17 (In thousands)	-	459	499	514	529	529	-	-	-	-
Men Ages 18–22 (In thousands)	-	430	450.4	478	505	505	-	-	-	-
MANPOWER										
Total Active	35,100	38,000	35,500	35,000	35,000	35,000	35,000	35,300	35,300	35,800
(Conscripts)	27,000	26,400	26,400	23,400	23,400	23,400	23,400	22,700	22,700	22,000
Total Reserve	-	-	-	-	-	-	-	-	-	-
Total Active + Reserves	35,100	38,000	35,500	35,000	35,000	35,000	35,000	35,300	35,300	35,800
Paramilitary	9,500	13,500	23,000	12,000	12,000	12,000	12,000	12,000	12,000	12,000
LAND FORCES										
Active Manpower	30,000	30,000	27,000	27,000	27,000	27,000	27,000	27,000	27,000	27,000
(Conscripts)	26,000	25,000	25,000	23,400	22,000	22,000	22,000	22,000	22,000	22,000
Reserve Manpower	-	-	-	-	-	-	-	-	-	-
Total Manpower	30,000	30,000	27,000	27,000	27,000	27,000	27,000	27,000	27,000	27,000
Main Battle Tanks	68	98	84	84	84	84	84	84	84	84
AIFVs/Armored Cars/Lt. Tanks	110	139	114	114	123	54	54	48	48	48
APCs/Recces/Scouts/Half-Tracks	68	208	268	268	337	327	327	328	328	328
ATGM Launchers	-	-	565	565	600	600	600	590	590	590

(continued)

Figure 5.1 *(continued)*

Category/Weapon	1985	1990	1995	2000	2002	2004	2005	2006	2007	2008
SP Artillery	54	28	0	0	0	0	0	0	0	0
Towed Artillery	83	123	117	117	117	117	117	115	115	115
MRLs	0	0	0	0	0	0	0	0	0	0
Mortars	-	-	135	161	155	191	191	161	161	161
SSM Launchers	-	0	0	0	0	0	0	0	0	0
AA Guns	-	-	115	115	115	115	115	127	127	127
Lt. SAM Launchers	-	-	73+	73+	73+	74	74	86	86	86
AIR AND AIR DEFENSE FORCES										
Active Manpower	2,500	3,500	3,500	3,500	3,500	3,500	3,500	3,500	3,500	4,000
Reserve Manpower	-	-	-	-	-	-	-	-	-	-
Aircraft										
Total Fighters/FGA/Recces	20	50	32	44	51	29	29	27	27	27
Bombers	0	0	0	0	0	0	0	0	0	0
Fighters	0	0	0	0	0	0	0	0	0	0
FGA	12	19	15	15	15	12	12	15	15	15
Recces	0	0	0	0	0	0	0	0	0	0
COIN/OCU	8	11	5	5	5	5	5	6	6	6
Airborne Early Warning (AEW)	0	0	0	0	0	0	0	0	0	0
Electronic Warfare (EW)	0	0	0	0	0	0	0	0	0	0
Maritime Reconnaissance	0	0	0	0	0	0	0	0	0	0
Combat-Capable Trainers	7	-	23	25	24	0	0	0	0	0
Tankers	0	0	0	0	0	0	0	0	0	0
Transport	6	4	7	11	13	16	16	20	20	20
HELICOPTERS										
Attack/Armed/ASW	1	0	7	7	7	15	15	12	12	12

(continued)

Figure 5.1 *(continued)*

Category/Weapon	1985	1990	1995	2000	2002	2004	2005	2006	2007	2008
Other	49	0	35	37	38	43	43	43	31	31
Total	50	41	42	44	45	58	58	55	43	43
SAM Forces										
Batteries	0	0	0	0	0	0	0	0	0	0
Heavy Launchers	0	0	0	0	0	0	0	0	0	0
NAVAL FORCES										
Active Manpower	2,600	4,500	5,000	4,500	4,500	4,500	4,500	4,800	4,800	4,800
Reserve Manpower	-	-	-	-	-	-	-	-	-	-
Total Manpower	-	-	-	-	-	-	-	-	-	-
Submarines	0	0	0	0	0	0	0	0	0	0
Destroyers/Frigates/Corvettes	1	1	0	0	0	0	0	0	0	0
Missile	0	0	0	0	0	0	0	0	0	0
Other	1	1	0	0	0	0	0	0	0	0
Missile Patrol	2	6	6	6	6	6	6	12	12	12
Coastal/Inshore Patrol	17	14	17	14	13	13	13	13	13	13
Mine	-	0	0	0	0	0	0	0	0	0
Amphibious Ships	-	0	0	0	0	0	0	0	0	0
Landing Craft/Light Support	-	-	-	3	2	2	2	2	2	6
ASW/Combat Helicopters	-	0	0	0	0	0	0	0	0	0

Source: Adapted by Anthony H. Cordesman from data provided by U.S. experts and from the International Institute for Strategic Studies, *The Military Balance*, various editions.

Note: Figures in parentheses are additional equipment in storage or not operational. SSM launchers are major systems. Main battle tank totals as of 2002 do not include units in storage. The numbers for attack/armed/ASW helicopters include UH-1H/Ns. The numbers for COIN/OCU include MB-326K/Ls. "O" connotes that a zero number has been verified, whereas "-" connotes that data are not known or verifiable.

6

FUTURE PATTERNS IN MILITARY DEVELOPMENT

The irony behind the problems in Maghreb military effectiveness is that it is unclear whether they really matter all that much to the nations concerned. The Maghreb countries have no real foreign enemies or strategic interests at stake, and the future patterns of security in the Maghreb depend more on internal and border area stability and the health of each economy than on strategic goals, military doctrine, and force plans. These realities help explain several of the most probable trends in military developments both in the region and in each country:

- The Maghreb states are likely to continue expanding their internal security forces and modernizing some of their major weapons in spite of diminished military requirements. This expansion will largely be the result of continuing internal and external political tension, bureaucratic momentum, and demographic pressure. Once the expansion of military forces takes place in a less-developed country, it has a powerful ratchet effect that has nothing to do with local threats or military requirements. The lack of alternative employment and career paths, coupled with the role of the military in the nation's power structure and the sheer momentum of global military expansion and technological change, leads to military expansion almost regardless of local political conditions.

- Morocco's forces are more than able to limit the Polisario threat to militarily, politically, and economically acceptable levels. Morocco should also be able to maintain adequate relations with Algeria despite both countries' increasing orders for new major combat systems. There is no guarantee that this will happen, however, and in light of what could be a new arms race, it is impossible to categorically rule out a long-term return to conflict between Algeria and Morocco, however unlikely that may be.

- Libya will continue its failure to properly man and modernize its military forces in spite of the suspension of UN sanctions in 1999 and a lifting of arms export bans on this former pariah state. Libya's suspension of its nuclear ambitions was a major shift in the regional balance, and may take some of the pressure off of the other states in the region to maintain higher levels of military spending than they desire.

- Algeria and Libya are experiencing steadily growing problems with obsolescence. Much of their equipment is worn, aging, improperly maintained, and difficult to support. The end result has been a steady decline in the operational readiness of older types of equipment and growing problems in supporting the overall force mix in combat. Both states are likely to drop in net military effectiveness even though they may acquire enough equipment to have an apparent increase in force strength. Algeria may have a head start in terms of new major orders, but it remains to be seen how Algeria will integrate and make use of its new acquisitions through 2010.

- The tensions within each country's military forces make military politics more important than military effectiveness. In Algeria, the army does not serve the country—it owns the country. The army suspended elections in 1992 in order to deny Islamic fundamentalists political control of the country. As a result, Algeria was engaged in a confusing, bloody internal conflict between the military government and Islamic extremists for more than a decade. Morocco's war with the Polisario now ties down its military and has led to significant economic strains. In 1987, a civil regime took over power from Bourguiba in Tunisia, but the continued incompetence and profiteering of the civil authorities may have laid the groundwork for an eventual military or radical Islamic takeover. Qadhafi has reportedly purged the Libyan military, but the military is virtually the only body that could replace him. Qadhafi has endured numerous coup attempts.

- The end of the Cold War has effectively ended the threat of communism and Soviet penetration into the region's military forces. Islamic fundamentalism and al Qaeda–inspired groups represent the greatest threat of instability to the secular and regular military forces in Algeria, Egypt, Libya, Morocco, and Tunisia.

- Creeping proliferation is likely to remain a problem. Algeria and Libya took steps to acquire WMD in the past, and Libya has had chemical weapons. This proliferation, however, is now severely constrained by funding problems and limited access to technology. Libya's suspension and rollback of its nuclear, biological, and chemical programs is a major step in the region.

MAJOR TRENDS IN MAGHREB MILITARY FORCES

The trends in the strength of Maghreb military forces become clearer when they are examined by major category of military strength. The data on manpower have already been discussed.

- **Figures 6.1** and **6.2** display the trends in armor, tanks, and artillery in the Maghreb. (Figures 6.1–6.15 appear at the end of this chapter.) As **Figure 6.1** shows, Libya possesses more than 5,000 armored vehicles (although some 1,040 tanks are in storage and useless), Algeria has more than 2,600, Morocco has more than 2,000, and Tunisia has more than 400. These inventory figures provide a rough indication of the amount of armor that any given force can bring to bear, although Libya can operate only a comparatively small portion of the armor it holds, other nations hold an unknown amount of this armor in storage, and North African armies are not organized to deploy and support massed armored forces.

- **Figures 6.2** through **6.4** show the number and type of tanks in each country. Algeria and Libya have the largest holdings, but the disparities in operational tanks are not as great as the total inventory data might indicate. Libya has more operational tanks on paper, but given upkeep limitations and the lack of spare parts, Algeria and Libya have rough parity in operational tanks. Morocco has more than two-thirds as many tanks as Algeria, and Tunisia has less than 100. Egypt has about four times more modern operational tanks than the largest North African power, and these include 850 M-60A3 and 755 M-1A1 tanks. Morocco has a comparatively large percentage of relatively modern M-60A3s, but also some 220 older M-60A1s. The 325 T-72s in Algerian forces and 200 in Libyan forces are roughly comparable to the M-60A3 in quality. However, the export version proved to be far more vulnerable in the Gulf War than many experts had previously estimated and suffer from a lack of modern fire-control systems.

- **Figure 6.5** compares the number of armored fighting vehicles. Morocco has large holdings, but also has large numbers of different types that are difficult to support. Algeria and Libya also have large holdings and reflect better standardization of equipment types, but also have large holdings of BMP-1s. The BMP-1 has proven to be more vulnerable than was initially estimated and to have poor war-fighting ergonomics.

- **Figures 6.6** and **6.7** indicate that Libya owns more than 1,900 pieces of artillery, Algeria has more than 680, Morocco has 352, and Tunisia has 115. Egypt's totals reflect considerably less emphasis on artillery than on armor. The totals for SP weapons provide a rough indication of the capability to carry out combined arms maneuvers and to rapidly deploy artillery to a new sector of a front. Algeria and Morocco have moderate to good SP artillery strength relative to their armor. The figures for Libya reflect total inventories. Once again, many of these holdings are in storage and Libya only has the manpower and support capabilities to fight a fraction of its total holdings.

- **Figures 6.8** through **6.11** display data on combat aircraft, armed helicopters, and EW aircraft. Libya has 374 fixed-wing aircraft and 35 armed helicopters. Algeria has 141 fixed-wing aircraft and 33 armed helicopters, Morocco has 89 and 19, and Tunisia has 27 and 12, respectively. As **Figures 6.9** through **6.11** show, however, the Maghreb countries have limited numbers of modern combat aircraft and relatively few reconnaissance, air control and warning, and EW aircraft. Algeria and Morocco are the only countries now actively modernizing this portion of their military forces, although Algeria may have a head start.

Morocco and Tunisia have no true high-performance combat aircraft. Libya has six aging Su-24s, and the rest of its holdings are much older 1970s and 1980s designs, and many are inactive or in storage. Egypt, in contrast, has a force of 119 modern F-16C/Ds, plus 38 F-16A/Bs and 15 Mirage 2000s. It is the only power neighboring the region with airborne battle-management assets and anything approaching modern electronic air warfare capabilities. The large air orders of battle of Algeria and Libya conceal what is becoming a technological museum.

- **Figure 6.12** shows the strength of land-based air defense forces. Libya has a large quantity of major and light SAM launchers and 490 AA guns. Algeria has SA-2, SA-3, and SA-6 major SAMs and 875 AA guns. Morocco and Tunisia have significantly smaller amounts of SAMs and AA guns. Almost all of these weapons systems are obsolescent or obsolete, however, and no North African state has a modern system of sensors, battle-management systems, airborne early warning, and integrated air/land-based command and control systems to operate and support its SAM systems.

- **Figures 6.13** and **6.14** display the total naval ship strength in North African forces. The number of ships in inventory, however, provides only a limited picture of comparative ship quality and war-fighting capability. A country-by-country analysis shows that many ships are poorly modernized and weaponized and have uncertain operational status or are inactive. Libya, in particular, has many ships that are in reserve to the point at which it is questionable whether they will ever be active again or are actually little more than hulks. Most North African combat ships have had little modernization, their air defense capabilities are weak, and their anti-ship missile defenses are very poor. No North African navy can currently operate as coherent fleets or task forces or in effective joint operations. Efforts are underway to correct this imbalance, with Algeria and Morocco looking to upgrade their fleets of major surface vessels, whereas Libya continues to look to its inshore and coastal capabilities.

- **Figure 6.15** shows the strength of the Polisario forces challenging Morocco in Western Sahara. These forces are small compared to the totals for Morocco. At the same time, Morocco cannot attack them systematically in their relative sanctuary in southern Algeria and must defend a vast territory. This presents a military challenge in spite of an extensive barrier defense system and Morocco's massive advantage in force numbers.

Taken together, these figures and tables provide a good picture of the overall military balance in the region, to the extent that such a balance exists. The figures dealing with equipment types also show the obsolescence of much of the Maghreb's military forces. The discussion above and the accompanying tables and figures also show the end result of a failed military buildup in Algeria and Libya and of decades of low-intensity war in Morocco. While Algeria and Morocco make a bid to acquire new systems and Libya makes a return to the global arms bazaar, only Tunisia has been relatively immune to the region's tragedy of arms.

Figure 6.1 Total North African Armor, 2008

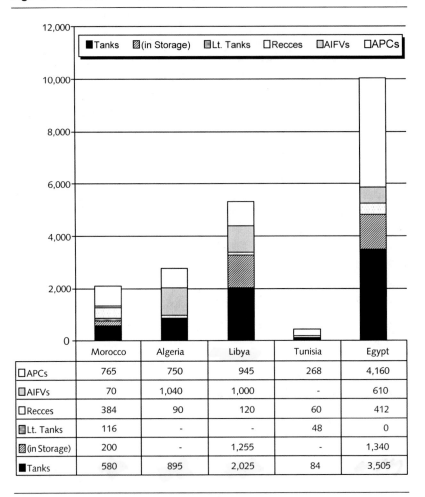

	Morocco	Algeria	Libya	Tunisia	Egypt
☐APCs	765	750	945	268	4,160
☐AIFVs	70	1,040	1,000	-	610
☐Recces	384	90	120	60	412
▨Lt. Tanks	116	-	-	48	0
▨(in Storage)	200	-	1,255	-	1,340
■Tanks	580	895	2,025	84	3,505

Source: Adapted by Anthony H. Cordesman from the International Institute for Strategic Studies, *The Military Balance*, various editions. "0" connotes that a zero number has been verified, whereas "-" connotes that data are not known or verifiable

Figure 6.2 Total North African Main Battle Tanks, 2008

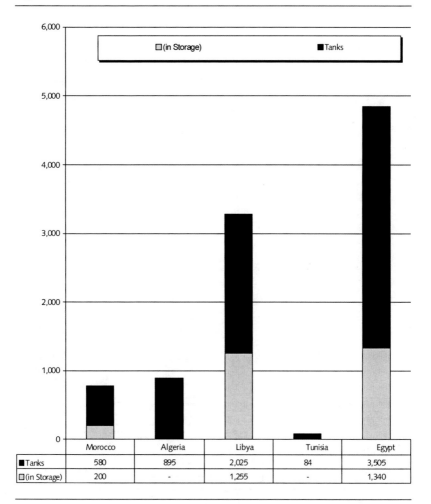

	Morocco	Algeria	Libya	Tunisia	Egypt
■Tanks	580	895	2,025	84	3,505
□(in Storage)	200	-	1,255	-	1,340

Source: Adapted by Anthony H. Cordesman from the International Institute for Strategic Studies, *The Military Balance*, various editions. "-" connotes that data are not known or verifiable.

Figure 6.3 Total North African Medium-Quality Active Main Battle Tanks by Type, 2008

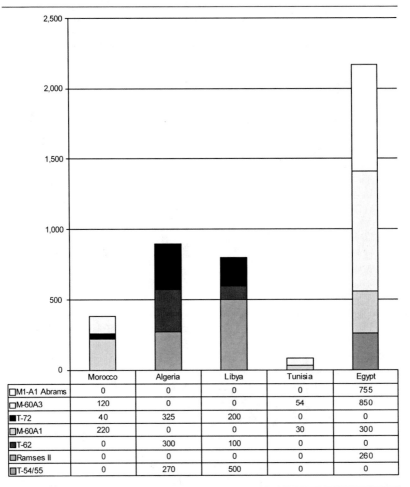

	Morocco	Algeria	Libya	Tunisia	Egypt
☐M1-A1 Abrams	0	0	0	0	755
☐M-60A3	120	0	0	54	850
■T-72	40	325	200	0	0
☐M-60A1	220	0	0	30	300
■T-62	0	300	100	0	0
☐Ramses II	0	0	0	0	260
☐T-54/55	0	270	500	0	0

Source: Adapted by Anthony H. Cordesman from the International Institute for Strategic Studies, *The Military Balance,* various editions.

Figure 6.4 Total North African Medium-Quality and Modern Active Main Battle Tanks, 2008

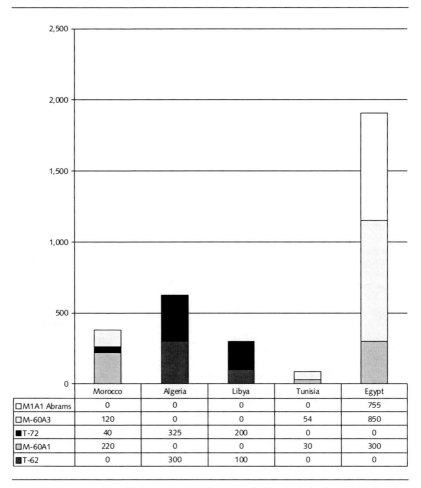

	Morocco	Algeria	Libya	Tunisia	Egypt
□M1A1 Abrams	0	0	0	0	755
□M-60A3	120	0	0	54	850
■T-72	40	325	200	0	0
□M-60A1	220	0	0	30	300
■T-62	0	300	100	0	0

Source: Adapted by Anthony H. Cordesman from the International Institute for Strategic Studies, *The Military Balance*, various editions.

Figure 6.5 Total North African Medium-Quality and Modern Other Armored Fighting Vehicles, 2008 (Less APCs)

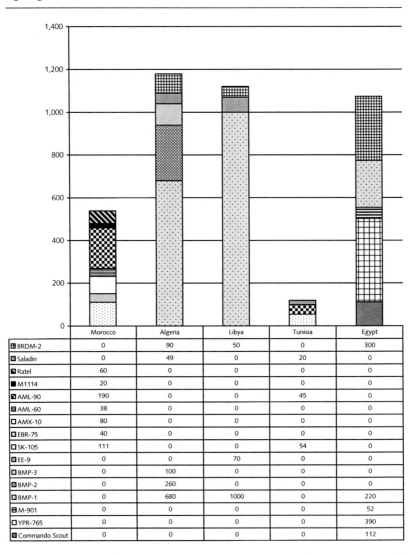

	Morocco	Algeria	Libya	Tunisia	Egypt
BRDM-2	0	90	50	0	300
Saladin	0	49	0	20	0
Ratel	60	0	0	0	0
M1114	20	0	0	0	0
AML-90	190	0	0	45	0
AML-60	38	0	0	0	0
AMX-10	80	0	0	0	0
EBR-75	40	0	0	0	0
SK-105	111	0	0	54	0
EE-9	0	0	70	0	0
BMP-3	0	100	0	0	0
BMP-2	0	260	0	0	0
BMP-1	0	680	1000	0	220
M-901	0	0	0	0	52
YPR-765	0	0	0	0	390
Commando Scout	0	0	0	0	112

Source: Adapted by Anthony H. Cordesman from the International Institute for Strategic Studies, *The Military Balance,* various editions.
Note: Totals include Egyptian BMP-1s in storage. "0" connotes that a zero number has been verified, whereas "-" connotes that data are not known or verifiable

Figure 6.6 Total North African Artillery, 2008

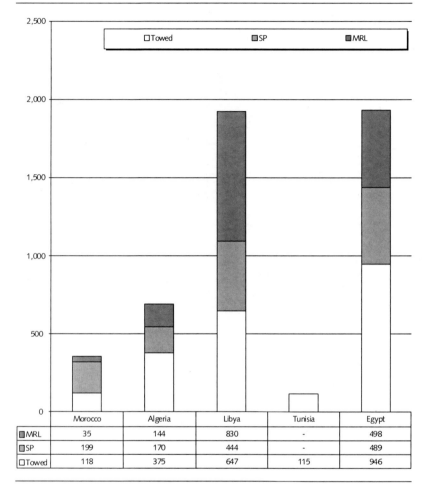

	Morocco	Algeria	Libya	Tunisia	Egypt
▣MRL	35	144	830	-	498
▣SP	199	170	444	-	489
☐Towed	118	375	647	115	946

Legend: ☐Towed   ▣SP   ▣MRL

Source: Adapted by Anthony H. Cordesman from the International Institute for Strategic Studies, *The Military Balance,* various editions.
Note: "-" connotes that data are not known or verifiable.

Figure 6.7 North African Self-Propelled Artillery, 2008

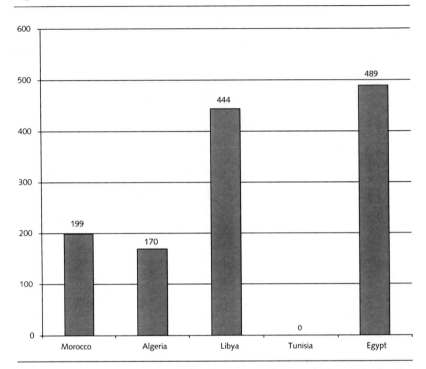

Source: Adapted by Anthony H. Cordesman from the International Institute for Strategic Studies, *The Military Balance*, various editions

Figure 6.8 North African Fixed-Wing Combat Aircraft and Armed Helicopters, 2008

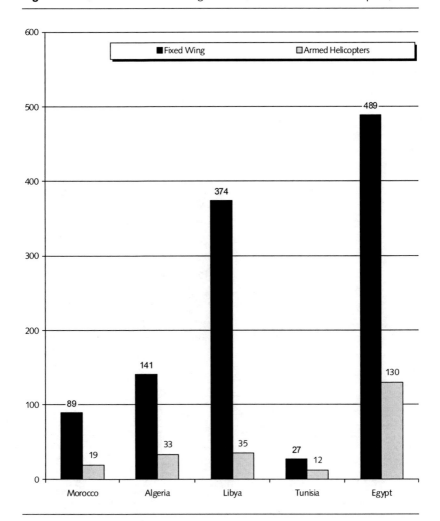

Source: Adapted by Anthony H. Cordesman from the International Institute for Strategic Studies, *The Military Balance,* various editions.
Note: Totals include all combat-capable, fixed-wing aircraft.

Figure 6.9 North African Active Bomber, Fighter, Fighter Ground Attack, and Strike Combat Aircraft by Type, 2008

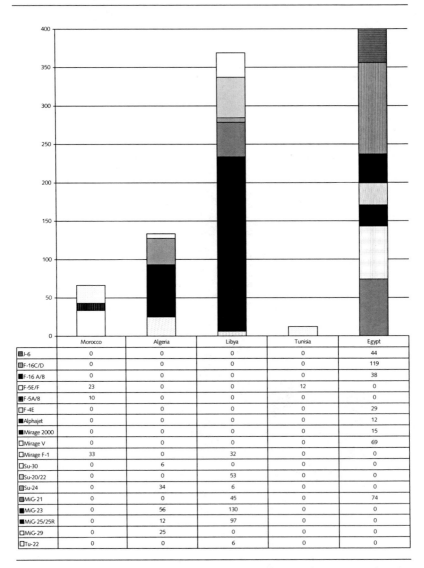

	Morocco	Algeria	Libya	Tunisia	Egypt
J-6	0	0	0	0	44
F-16C/D	0	0	0	0	119
F-16 A/B	0	0	0	0	38
F-5E/F	23	0	0	12	0
F-5A/B	10	0	0	0	0
F-4E	0	0	0	0	29
Alphajet	0	0	0	0	12
Mirage 2000	0	0	0	0	15
Mirage V	0	0	0	0	69
Mirage F-1	33	0	32	0	0
Su-30	0	6	0	0	0
Su-20/22	0	0	53	0	0
Su-24	0	34	6	0	0
MiG-21	0	0	45	0	74
MiG-23	0	56	130	0	0
MiG-25/25R	0	12	97	0	0
MiG-29	0	25	0	0	0
Tu-22	0	0	6	0	0

Source: Adapted by Anthony H. Cordesman from the International Institute for Strategic Studies, *The Military Balance*, various editions.
Note: Does not include stored, unarmed electronic warfare, or combat-capable Recces and trainer aircraft.

Figure 6.10 North African Medium- and High-Quality Combat Aircraft by Type, 2008

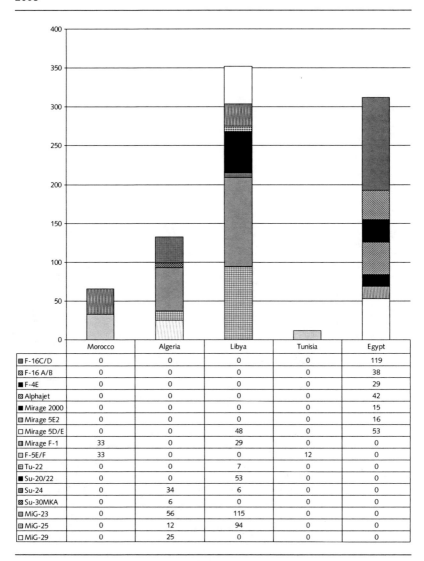

	Morocco	Algeria	Libya	Tunisia	Egypt
▣ F-16C/D	0	0	0	0	119
▨ F-16 A/B	0	0	0	0	38
▮ F-4E	0	0	0	0	29
▨ Alphajet	0	0	0	0	42
▪ Mirage 2000	0	0	0	0	15
▤ Mirage 5E2	0	0	0	0	16
▢ Mirage 5D/E	0	0	48	0	53
▣ Mirage F-1	33	0	29	0	0
▢ F-5E/F	33	0	0	12	0
⊞ Tu-22	0	0	7	0	0
▪ Su-20/22	0	0	53	0	0
▣ Su-24	0	34	6	0	0
▨ Su-30MKA	0	6	0	0	0
▣ MiG-23	0	56	115	0	0
⊞ MiG-25	0	12	94	0	0
▢ MiG-29	0	25	0	0	0

Source: Adapted by Anthony H. Cordesman from the International Institute for Strategic Studies, *The Military Balance,* various editions.

Note: Does not include stored, unarmed electronic warfare, or combat-capable Recces and trainer aircraft. "0" connotes that a zero number has been verified, whereas "-" connotes that data are not known or verifiable.

Figure 6.11 North African Active AEW, ELINT, and EW Aircraft by Type, 2008

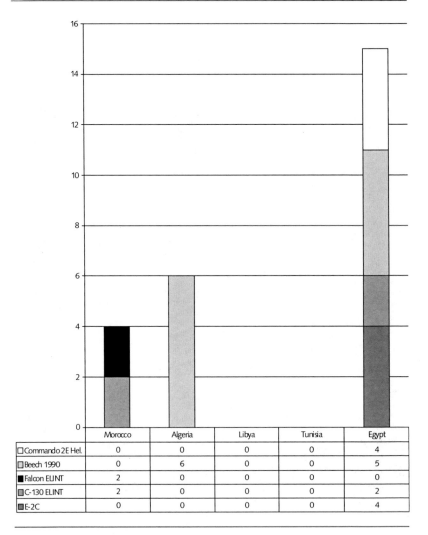

	Morocco	Algeria	Libya	Tunisia	Egypt
☐ Commando 2E Hel.	0	0	0	0	4
☐ Beech 1990	0	6	0	0	5
■ Falcon ELINT	2	0	0	0	0
▨ C-130 ELINT	2	0	0	0	2
▨ E-2C	0	0	0	0	4

Source: Adapted by Anthony H. Cordesman from the International Institute for Strategic Studies, *The Military Balance*, various editions.
Note: Does not include Recces or dedicated maritime reconnaissance aircraft.

Figure 6.12 North African Land-Based Air Defenses, 2008

Country	Major SAM	Light SAM	AA Guns
Morocco	None	37 M-48 Chaparral 70 SA-7 Grail	407 guns: 150–180 ZPU-2 14.5-mm 20 ZPU-4 14.5-mm 40 M-167 Vulcan 20-mm 75–90 ZU-23-2 23-mm 17 KS-19 100-mm
Algeria	140 SA-2, 3, 6,	220 SA-7, SA-14, SA-16 48 SA-8 20 SA-9	875 guns: 225 ZSU-23-4 60 ZPU-2 14.5-mm 40 ZPU-4 14.5-mm 100 ZPU-2/4 20-mm 100 ZU-23 23-mm 100 M-1939 37-mm 70 S-60 57-mm 20 M-1939 KS-12 85-mm 150 KS-19 100-mm 10 KS-30 130-mm
Libya	5-6 bde/18 SA-2 2-3 bde/12 SA-3 4 bde SA-5 3 bde/20-24 SA-6 72 SP SA-6	400 SA-7 SA-9 SA-13 24 Quad Crotale 50 L/70 40-mm	490+ guns: 250 ZSU-23-4 23-mm 100 ZPU-2 14.5-mm M-53/59 30-mm 90 S-60 57-mm
Tunisia	None	60 RBS-70 26 M-48 Chaparral	127 guns: 12 M-42 40-mm 100 M-55 20-mm 15 Type-55/65 37-mm
Egypt	110 bn/212 SA-3/6 282+ SA-2 Guideline 12 bty/78+ I-Hawk	2000+ SA-7/FIM-92A Stinger 282+ Skyguard 76+ M-48/M-54 Chaparral RIM-7F 36 quad SAM Ayn as Saqr 24+ Cortale	705+ guns 45 Sinai-23 23-mm 120 ZSU-23-4 23-mm 40 ZSU-57-2 57-mm 300 ZPU-4 14.5-mm 200 ZU-23-2 23-mm S-60 57-mm

Source: Adapted by Anthony H. Cordesman from the International Institute for Strategic Studies, *The Military Balance*, various editions; *Jane's Sentinel*, various editions.
Note: Air defense data total includes SAM and gun totals under army and air defense commands. Abbreviations: bde = brigade; bn = battalion; bty = battery.

Figure 6.13 North African Naval Ships in Active Inventory by Category, 2008

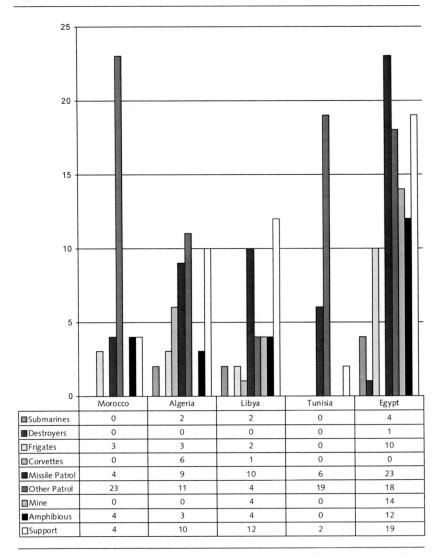

	Morocco	Algeria	Libya	Tunisia	Egypt
Submarines	0	2	2	0	4
Destroyers	0	0	0	0	1
Frigates	3	3	2	0	10
Corvettes	0	6	1	0	0
Missile Patrol	4	9	10	6	23
Other Patrol	23	11	4	19	18
Mine	0	0	4	0	14
Amphibious	4	3	4	0	12
Support	4	10	12	2	19

Source: Adapted by Anthony H. Cordesman from the International Institute for Strategic Studies, *The Military Balance*, various editions; *Jane's Fighting Ships*, various editions.

Figure 6.14 North African Major Active Combat Ships, 2008

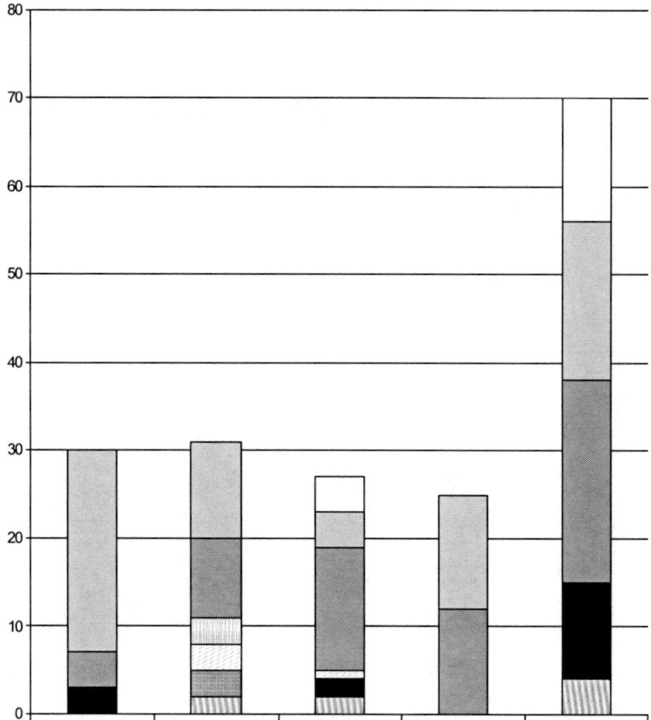

	Morocco	Algeria	Libya	Tunisia	Egypt
☐ Mine	0	0	4	0	14
☐ Other Ocean & Coastal Patrol	23	11	4	13	18
▨ Missile Patrol	4	9	14	12	23
☐ Other Corvettes	0	3	0	0	0
☐ Guided Missile Corvettes	0	3	1	0	0
▨ Other Frigates	0	3	0	0	0
■ Guided Missile Frigates	3	0	2	0	10
■ Other Destroyers	0	0	0	0	1
▨ Guided Missile Destroyers	0	0	0	0	0
▨ Submarines	0	2	2	0	4

Source: Adapted by Anthony H. Cordesman from the International Institute for Strategic Studies, *The Military Balance*, various editions; *Jane's Fighting Ships*, various editions.

Figure 6.15 Polisario Forces: Manpower, Weapons, and Equipment

Manpower

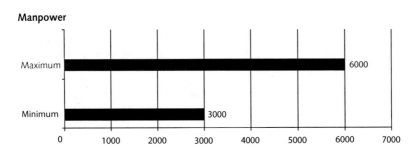

Weapons Manpower

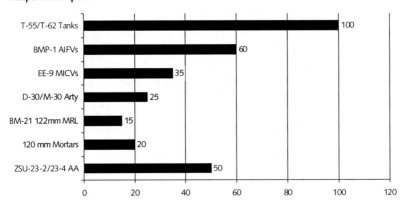

Other Equipment

- Steyr SK-105 light tanks
- Panhard APCs
- Ratel 20 AFVs
- Eland armored reconnaissance vehicles
- AML-90s
- AT-3 Sagger anti-tank guided missiles
- SA-6, SA-7, SA-8, and SA-9 surface-to-air missiles

Source: Adapted by Anthony H. Cordesman from data provided by U.S. experts; the International Institute for Strategic Studies, *The Military Balance,* various editions; *and Jane's Sentinel,* various editions.

Note: Polisario also known as Sahrawi People's Liberation Army. Manpower and weapons manpower based on past estimates, no longer current. Other equipment numbers unknown.

ABOUT THE AUTHORS

Anthony H. Cordesman holds the Arleigh A. Burke Chair in Strategy at CSIS. He is also a national security analyst for ABC News. He has served as national security assistant to Senator John McCain on the Senate Armed Services Committee, as director of intelligence assessment in the Office of the Secretary of Defense, and as a civilian assistant to the deputy secretary of defense. He has also held positions at the Department of State, Department of Energy, and NATO International Staff. His numerous foreign assignments include postings in Lebanon, Egypt, and Iran, and he has worked extensively in Saudi Arabia and the Gulf. Cordesman is the author of more than 50 books, including *Iraq's Insurgency and the Road to Civil Conflict* (Praeger, 2007), *Lessons of the 2006 Israeli-Hezbollah War* (CSIS, 2007), *Iran's Military Forces and Warfighting Capabilities* (Praeger, 2007), *Salvaging American Defense* (Praeger, 2007), and *Iran's Weapons of Mass Destruction* (CSIS, 2006). He is a former adjunct professor of national security studies at Georgetown University and has twice been a fellow at the Woodrow Wilson International Center.

Aram Nerguizian is a research assistant at the Burke Chair in Strategy, where he works on projects concerning the Middle East and North Africa. His research focuses on security politics in the Levant and the Gulf with an emphasis on specialized themes, such as the Lebanese Armed Forces' efforts to recapitalize its forces in the post-Syria era. Nerguizian holds a master's degree from the George Washington University's Elliott School of International Affairs.